ONE PEOPLE

ONE PEOPLE

John R. W. Stott

Inter-Varsity Press
Downers Grove, Illinois 60515

Second printing, March 1971

Biblical quotations are from the
Revised Standard Version, copyright 1946 and 1952.

© 1968 by John R. W. Stott

First American printing, September 1970
by Inter-Varsity Press with permission
from the Church Pastoral-Aid Society,
London, England
All rights reserved

Inter-Varsity Press is the book
publishing division of
Inter-Varsity Christian Fellowship.

SBN 0-87784-694-4
Library of Congress Catalog Card Number: 72-127931

Printed in the United States of America

Contents

Author's Preface

THIS little book is a revision and expansion of the Pastoral Theology lectures delivered in Durham University in February 1968. I am very grateful to the Divinity Faculty for inviting me to give this annual series of lectures, and specially to Professor H. E. W. Turner and Canon J. Hickinbotham for their personal encouragement.

The title proposed to me for the lectures was 'The Theology of the Laity'. Since they were prepared in the first instance for theological students, it is natural that I kept in mind particularly the attitudes of the clergy to the laity. Nevertheless, in offering these thoughts to a wider public, I hope that they will not be read only by clergy (whether potential or actual). The whole question of clergy–laity relationships is of vital concern to both parties, in fact to the whole Church. Perhaps there is material here for consideration by parochial study groups and Parochial Church Councils. It is extremely important for the life and growth of the Church that relations between clergy and laity should be not only harmonious in practice, but biblical in principle.

Inevitably in writing I have drawn from my own parochial experience during the years that I have sought to serve the church and parish of All Souls, Langham Place, in London. If the personal references jar on the reader, I ask him to believe that their purpose is not self-advertisement, but a desire to 'earth' theories in an actual real-life situation. At the same time, I recognize that parochial life in central London is to some extent unusual (though less so than many suppose, since our parish's resident population is nearly 9,000). What matters most are the principles involved; their detailed application is bound to vary from place to place and from parish to parish.

I must ask forgiveness for the use of transliterated Greek words. I have retained them because it seems to me that Christian people ought to be familiar with some of the common words of the New Testament which have a particular flavour of their own. All of us nowadays include in our vocabulary words of Greek origin like antibiotic, psychosomatic medicine and stereophonic sound. We do not jib at them. School-children learn about photosynthesis in their botany lessons, journalists write about euphoria and syndromes, while Church leaders constantly talk about the eschatological significance of ecumenicity! So I hope words like *ecclesia, diakonia, marturia* and *koinonia* will not deter the reader, even if they are not yet in common parlance.

Note to American Readers

To American readers I have to apologise not only for the Greek terms but also for the English and Anglican allusions! I hope they will not be found distracting, because the principles I have tried to unfold are applicable to every denomination in every country. Nevertheless, let me explain two expressions.

The Parochial Church Council (or PCC), whose equivalent in the American Episopal Church is the 'Vestry', is the body responsible for the life and work of the local church. It consists of the clergy (ex officio) and a varying number of lay people elected at the Annual Parochial Church Meeting.

The 'Lambeth Conference' is a conference of the diocesan bishops of the Anglican Communion, held approximately every 10 years. The first was in 1888, and the post-war Conferences were held in 1948, 1958 and 1968.

The Resurgence of the Laity

LET me begin with three quotations.

First, from a Papal Encyclical, that of Pius x in 1906 entitled *Vehementer Nos*:

> As for the masses, they have no other right than that of letting themselves be led, and of following their pastors as a docile flock.

Next an Anglican assessment by Sir Kenneth Grubb:

> The Church of England does not give a strong impression of being interested in its laity: it seems either to ride them or to fear them.

And a rather sardonic addition:

> It seems a fair assumption . . . that the clergy of the Church of England do not trust the laity, and, if this be indeed so, then there is no strong reason why the laity should not return the compliment.[1]

Thirdly, an anonymous elegy, of no poetic merit, published in the St Marylebone Magazine in 1961 and composed (I have since learned) by the Rector's family:

> The Rector is late,
> He's forgotten the date,
> So what can the faithful do now,
> Poor things?
> They'll sit in a pew
> With nothing to do
> And sing a selection of hymns,
> Poor things!

If these quotations express at all accurately the Church's view of the laity, whether official or unofficial, whether recent or current, whether Roman or Anglican, we shall have no difficulty in agreeing with the following Lambeth 1958 statements: 'there

---

[1] Grubb: *A Layman Looks at the Church*, p. 161, 112

is a growing recognition today that too sharp a distinction has been made between clergy and laity'[1] and 'there is need for a better theology of the laity'.[2]

As a matter of fact, in every part of the Christian Church today the layman is coming into his own. There have been notable lay movements before, for example in the middle ages and at the Reformation; and the lay initiative which led to the founding of great international youth and missionary movements in the 19th century has not yet spent its force. But these were spontaneous, the upsurge of lay energy from below, sometimes tolerated by church leaders only because they had no alternative. Today, however, toleration is being superseded by encouragement, reluctance by enthusiasm. The layman is being taken seriously because there is a growing recognition of his true place in the Church.

Many reasons are given to justify the increasingly prominent position occupied by laymen in the contemporary Church. To begin with, there are the sociological facts of an increasing birth rate and a decreasing ordination rate. We can bring this alarming situation into focus by taking the two years 1851 and 1951. During this century the population of England, of the provinces of Canterbury and York, increased by nearly 25 million (from 16·9 to 41·3 million), while the number of clergy increased by only just 2,000 (from 16,194 to 18,196). The average age of the clergy during the same century jumped from 44 to 55. Fifteen years later still (in 1966) the population had grown by a further 4·4 million, but the number of clergy only by the pitiful figure of 48 (from 18,196 to 18,244). Between 1851 and 1966 there was a fall in the ratio of clergy to people from 1 in 1,000 to 1 in 2,500. This combination of more people and fewer parsons is a contributory factor in the current drift from the churches. It is also one reason why many overworked clergy, who previously held the parochial reins tightly in their own hands, are now being obliged to seek the help of the laity. Tom Allan refers to them as 'the unemployed of the Church',[3] but now many are being found employment. As Hendrik Kraemer puts it, the laity had before 'existed mainly as frozen credits'; now they are being unfrozen and put into circulation. We cannot stop there, however, for to borrow another of Kraemer's metaphors, the laity are 'not primarily an insufficiently tapped reservoir of man-power'.[4]

A second reason why lay people are being better trusted in the Church is the fear that if we do not give them – in this case specially the men – man-sized jobs to do, we shall lose them, at least in their spare time, to masonry or rotary or one of the secular voluntary services or even one of the sects, all of whom are better at giving responsible positions to men than most churches have ever been.[5] This is not to say that Christian men should not be involved in community service. They should. When such involvement is recognized as part of the Christian calling and has the supporting encouragement of the local church, it is good and right. But when it is undertaken only *faute de mieux*, from a sense of frustrated uselessness in the church, something has gone sadly wrong.

Canon Max Warren makes this point well.[6] He compares the revival movement in East Africa, which has stayed inside the Church, with the separatist groups in South Africa, of which he says there are more than 1,300. These have been described by Dr (now Bishop) B. G. M. Sundkler in his *Bantu Prophets in South Africa*, and from this study Canon Warren makes a number of significant points. The first is that 'it is impossible to condemn the African for being separatist when he is treated as a separated person'. He goes on:

The fact that in addition to being separated within the Church he was

[1] *The Lambeth Conference, 1958*, p. 1.26
[2] *The Lambeth Conference, 1958*, p. 2.99
[3] Allan: *The Face of my Parish*, p. 54
[4] Kraemer: *A Theology of the Laity*, pp. 34, 37
[5] Leslie Paul comments: 'the revealing fact is that the laity have seldom been used in the past, and are seldom used by the Church today, in church affairs at the level of their ability in secular affairs' (*Layman's Church*, p. 43)
[6] Warren: *Revival – An Enquiry*, p. 28

subordinated as well, and so was unable to exercise either initiative or authority, powerfully conduced to the act of formal separation.

Therefore

the problem of how to provide adequate scope for initiative and leadership, the problem of 'the layman' remains one of the more outstanding of the tasks confronting the Church in Africa.

– and indeed, one might add, throughout the world.

Thirdly, the Church has not escaped the effects of the social and political revolution which has engulfed the world in this century and brought maturity and a sense of responsibility to large numbers of ordinary citizens. Compulsory secondary education and the increasing availability of tertiary education, the spread of democracy and with it of universal adult suffrage, the emancipation of 'the workers' in both communist and capitalist forms, the trades' union movement, the global revolt against privilege, authoritarianism and every kind of establishment, and the insistence upon egalitarian rights are all straws in the same wind. To this modern outlook the Church often appears to be a redoubtable bastion of the old order, reactionary and resistant to change, while the Church's hierarchical structure seems to some like an antique relic of the feudalism which was otherwise discarded in the middle ages.

These are three pragmatic reasons for the greater participation of laymen in the life and work of the Church – need, fear and the spirit of the age. They are sound reasons too, so far as they go, but inadequate. The real reason for expecting the laity to be responsible, active and constructive church members is biblical not pragmatic, grounded on theological principle, not on expediency. It is neither because the clergy need the laity to help them, nor because the laity want to be of use, nor because the world now thinks this way, but because God Himself has revealed it as His will. Moreover, the only way in which the laity will come to see and accept their inalienable rights and duties in the Church is that they come to recognize them in the Word of God as the will of God for the people of God.

THE BIBLICAL ARGUMENT

We have already seen that it is impossible to talk about laity without also talking about clergy. We must now see that it is impossible to talk about either without talking about the Church to which they both belong. 'Fundamentally', wrote Yves Congar 'there can be only one valid theology of the laity: a total ecclesiology'.[1] It is safe to say that unbalanced notions about either clergy or laity are due to unbalanced notions of the Church. Indeed, to be more precise, too low a view of laity is due to too high a view of clergy, and too high a view of clergy is due to too low a view of the Church.

It may be helpful if at this stage I sketch out the ground which I hope to cover in this book.

In the first chapter we shall consider some of the main emphases in the biblical doctrine of the Church, the *Ecclesia*, particularly in connection with the relations between clergy and laity.

In the second chapter I shall try to outline the four kinds of relationship which at various times have existed between clergy and laity. I shall urge that clergy are called to ministry (*diakonia*), and that therefore the true and proper relationship of clergy to laity is a *serving* relationship.

In Chapter 3 this general principle will be worked out in detail and in practice. We shall see that the chief way in which the clergy are to serve the laity is in helping to teach and train them for their life, work and especially witness (*marturia*) in the world. In other words the *diakonia*, service, of the clergy is subservient to the *marturia* of the laity. In unfolding this theme, I will share with you some of our experience in London both of

[1] Yves M. J. Congar: *Lay People in the Church* (Geoffrey Chapman, 1957)

an annual Training School for the equipment of 'Commissioned Workers' and of their varied service in the parish. As I do so, I shall describe the scheme so far as possible through their eyes as well as mine, since I shall draw on their answers to a questionnaire submitted to them.

In the last chapter, we shall move on from the relations between clergy and laity to the wider field of the relations of church members to one another in the fellowship of the Church. I shall attempt to unfold what the Bible means by *koinonia*, fellowship, and to explore how it should be expressed in the local congregation. This will involve an examination of 'Fellowship Groups', both the biblical ideal and the actual reality.

The Christian Assembly *(ecclesia)*

THE question we must ask in this first chapter is: what is the Church?

The Church is a people, a community of people, who owe their existence, their solidarity and their corporate distinctness from other communities to one thing only – the call of God.

It all began with Abraham, called by God to leave his own country and kindred in order to be given another country and another kindred, in order to be made a great people through whom all peoples on earth would be blessed. Several times this covenant of grace was confirmed to Abraham, that through his descendants all earth's nations would be blessed.[1] It was then further confirmed to Abraham's son Isaac and to Isaac's son Jacob. But Jacob died in captivity. So did his distinguished son Joseph. Indeed Genesis ends with the prosaic information that after Joseph died, he was embalmed and 'put in a coffin in Egypt'.[2]

But there was a great leap forward in the fulfilment of God's promise when through Moses, descended from Jacob's son Levi, He rescued the people from their slavery. 'When Israel was a child, I loved him, and out of Egypt I called my son.'[3] Three months after the Exodus they entered the wilderness of Sinai, and the Lord told Moses to say to the people:

> You have seen . . . how I bore you on eagles' wings and brought you to myself. Now therefore, if you will obey my voice and keep my covenant, you shall be my own possession among all peoples; for all the earth is mine, and you shall be to me a kingdom of priests and a holy nation.[4]

---

[1] *for instance* Genesis 22.17–18
[2] Genesis 50.26
[3] Hosea 11.1
[4] Exodus 19.4–6

So the covenant was ratified, the law given, the tabernacle worship begun. Later the promised land was conquered, and later still the monarchy established. But it all ended in disaster. God's people broke His covenant, rejected His law and despised His prophets, until there was no remedy. The judgment of God fell upon them, and the second, the Babylonian captivity began.

Yet God did not abandon His people. In due course, true to His promise to bless them, He called them out of Babylon, as He had called them out of Egypt, and He restored them to their own land. As God said through Jeremiah:

> Therefore, behold, the days are coming, says the Lord, when it shall no longer be said, 'As the Lord lives who brought up the people of Israel out of the land of Egypt,' but 'As the Lord lives who brought up the people of Israel out of the north country and out of all the countries where he had driven them.' For I will bring them back to their own land which I gave to their fathers. [1]

But God had also promised through His people to bless all the nations of the earth. And this came to pass through Christ. For God's call into the land of Canaan first of Abraham's family from Ur and from Haran, then of Jacob's descendants from Egypt, and then of the remnant of Judah from Babylon all foreshadowed a better call, a greater redemption, and a richer inheritance. Through the death and resurrection of Christ, God's purpose is to call out of the world a people for Himself, to redeem them from sin, and to cause them to inherit His promises of salvation.

So the Church is God's people, His *ecclesia*, called out of the world to be His, and existing as a separate entity solely because of His call. The New Testament insists strongly upon this fact. God has called us 'into the fellowship of his Son Jesus Christ our Lord', called us 'to belong to Jesus Christ'. [2] This divine call is 'a holy calling', a calling 'in holiness'. [3] God calls us to be holy as He is holy, and 'to lead a life worthy of the calling' to which we have been called, [4] so that by the sanctifying power of the Holy Spirit we may become in character and conduct what we already are in status, namely 'saints', the holy, the distinct, the separate, the special people of God.[5]

But God's call is not intended to withdraw the Church out of the world into pietism. As Bishop Lesslie Newbigin puts it, 'the Church . . . is a community *in via*, on its way to the ends of the earth and to the end of time'. Again,

> the Church is the pilgrim people of God. It is on the move – hastening to the ends of the earth to beseech all men to be reconciled to God, and hastening to the end of time to meet its Lord who will gather all into one.

It is for this reason, he argues, that the Church 'cannot be understood rightly except in a perspective which is at once missionary and eschatological'.[6] So, the New Testament authors declare, the God who has called us out of the world sends us back into the world:

> you are a chosen race, a royal priesthood, a holy nation, God's own people, that you may declare the wonderful deeds of him who called you out of darkness into his marvellous light.[7]

He has also called us like Christ to suffer in the world unjustly, and through suffering He has called us 'to his eternal glory in Christ'.[8]

Such is the Church, God's people, called out of the world to Himself, called to holiness, called to mission, called to suffering, and called through suffering to glory.

GOD'S CHURCH IS ONE CHURCH

And this calling of the Church is the calling of the whole

---

[1] Jeremiah 16.14–15
[2] 1 Corinthians 1.9; Romans 1.6
[3] 2 Timothy 1.9; 1 Thessalonians 4.7
[4] *see* 1 Peter 1.15–16; Ephesians 4.1
[5] *for instance* Romans 1.7; 1 Corinthians 1.2; *see also* Acts 15.14; Titus 2.14
[6] Newbigin: *The Household of God*, p. 31, 25 – 'eschatological', derived from *eschatos* ('last') or *eschaton* ('end'), refers to the end of time and the last things, the consummation which lies behind history
[7] 1 Peter 2.9
[8] 1 Peter 2.20–21; 5.10

Church, and of every member of the Church, without any distinction or partiality. Previously, God's call had been to Abraham and his descendants, to physical, national Israel, and the Gentiles had been 'alienated from the commonwealth of Israel, and strangers to the covenants of promise'.[1] Yet the promise to Abraham included an ultimate blessing for all the nations. So Paul could write to the Ephesians:

> But now in Christ Jesus you who once were far off have been brought near in the blood of Christ. For he is our peace, who has made us both one, and has broken down the dividing wall of hostility, by abolishing in his flesh the law of commandments and ordinances, that he might create in himself one new man in place of the two, so making peace, and might reconcile us both to God in one body through the cross, thereby bringing the hostility to an end.[2]

We must not miss the apostle's reference to an abolition and a creation. God abolished that aspect of the law which made Israel a separate people, and He created 'one new man'.

And this one new humanity, which is the Church, is a marvellously comprehensive community. Christ has abolished more barriers than that of race or nationality; He has abolished those of class and sex as well: 'there is neither Jew nor Greek, there is neither slave nor free, there is neither male nor female: for you are all one in Christ Jesus'.[3] Thus the days of discrimination are over. The new humanity Christ has created in the Church tolerates no distinction of race, rank or sex. This does not mean that Christian equality is a synonym for anarchy, since the same apostle who asserts it also tells wives to be subject to their husbands and servants to their masters, but rather that all spiritual privilege before God has been eliminated:

> For there is no distinction . . . the same Lord is Lord of all and bestows his riches upon all who call upon him. For 'everyone who calls upon the name of the Lord will be saved'[4]

As a result all Christian believers, whether Jew or Gentile, male or female, slave or freeman, educated Greek or uncouth barbarian or Scythian, are 'fellow-citizens with the saints and members of the household of God', and again 'fellow-heirs, members of the same body, and partakers of the promise in Christ Jesus through the gospel'.[5] Paul's use in these verses of four Greek compounds which might be rendered 'fellow-citizens', 'fellow-heirs', 'fellow-members' and 'fellow-partakers'[6] enforces as clearly and strongly as any words could the undifferentiated, common participation of all God's people in all the blessings of the gospel. He is teaching the same truth in his catalogue of unities in Ephesians 4.4–6, that

> There is one body and one Spirit, just as you were called to the one hope that belongs to your call, one Lord, one faith, one baptism, one God and Father of us all, who is above all and through all and in all.

But what is the relevance of this to a book about the laity? Why have I thought it necessary to reassert this abolition of privilege and this creation of one new humanity with equal rights and equal privileges? For this reason: it is only against the background of the equality and unity of the people of God that the real scandal of clericalism may be seen. What clericalism always does, by concentrating power and privilege in the hands of the clergy, is at least to obscure and at worst to annul the essential oneness of the people of God. Extreme forms of clericalism dare to reintroduce the notion of privilege into the only human community in which it has been abolished. Where Christ has made out of two one, the clerical mind makes two again, the one higher and the other lower, the one active and the other passive, the one really important because vital to the life of the Church, the other not vital and therefore less important. I do not hesitate to say that to interpret the Church

---

[1] Ephesians 2.12
[2] Ephesians 2.13–16
[3] Galatians 3.28
[4] Romans 10.12–13
[5] Colossians 3.11; Ephesians 2.19; 3.6
[6] No English translation can do justice to the striking Greek compounds *sumpolitai*, fellow-citizens; *sugkleronoma*, fellow-heirs; *sussoma*, fellow-members, and *summetocha*, fellow-partakers

in terms of a privileged clerical caste or hierarchical structure is to destroy the New Testament doctrine of the Church.

But we have no liberty to interpret 'Church' in terms of 'clergy', however easy it is for the clerical mind to lapse into this way of thinking. In order to demonstrate this, we shall review some of the chief biblical images of the Church. These are many and varied, and rich in implication. We cannot submit them to an exhaustive examination, but we can consider them with sufficient care to establish this point: every biblical image of the Church illumines the relations of God's people to Himself in Christ and/or to each other. Little if any attention is paid to the clergy as a third party distinct from either. In other words, in revealing the nature and work of the Church, the over-whelming preoccupation of the New Testament is not with the status of the clergy, nor with clergy–laity relations, but with the whole people of God in their relations to Him and to each other, the unique people who have been called by His grace to be His inheritance and His ambassador in the world.

METAPHORS OF THE CHURCH

Three of the most picturesque images of the Church are taken over by the New Testament from the Old. They represent God's people as His bride, His vineyard and His flock. They all highlight the direct relationship which God has established with His people and which they enjoy with Him.

God looked upon Israel in her maidenhood, betrothed her to Himself as His bride and entered into a marriage covenant with her.[1] He then had to keep complaining of her unfaithfulness, her acts of adultery and even her promiscuity.[2]

God brought a vine out of Egypt and planted it in Canaan, 'a very fertile hill'. There it took root and filled the land. He built a watchtower from which to guard it and a wine-vat to prepare for the vintage. And He looked for it to yield grapes of righteousness, but it yielded only the wild grapes of injustice and oppression. So He made His vineyard a waste.[3]

Again, God was the Shepherd of Israel. He led Joseph like a flock. As He had redeemed them from Egypt, 'lifted them up and carried them all the days of old', so after the Babylonian captivity He would gather the lambs in His arms and gently lead those with young.[4]

Each image stresses God's direct and purposeful dealings with His people as a people, His sovereign, saving initiative towards them. He chose Israel as His bride, He planted His vineyard, He shepherded His flock. And when Jesus boldly reapplied the metaphors to Himself, He emphasized even more strongly the personal relationship which each implied.

He was the Bridegroom, whose presence with the wedding guests made fasting inappropriate.[5] Paul developed the metaphor in greater detail with reference to Christ's loving self-sacrifice for the Church, His headship over her and His final purpose for her, that she should be presented before Him 'in splendour, without spot or wrinkle or any such thing'.[6] At the end of the Revelation we first hear that 'the marriage of the Lamb has come and his Bride has made herself ready' and then see 'the holy city, new Jerusalem, coming down out of heaven from God, prepared as a bride adorned for her husband'.[7]

Jesus took up the image of the vineyard in his Parable of the Wicked Husbandmen,[8] but He also extended it, for He claimed to be the Vine itself, whose branches were dependent for their fruitfulness both on their abiding in Him and on their being pruned by the vinedresser.[9]

And Jesus called Himself 'the Good Shepherd', going out into

---

[1] *For instance* Ezekiel 16; Jeremiah 2.2; 31.32; Isaiah 62.5
[2] *For instance* Hosea 2
[3] Psalm 80.8–19; Isaiah 5
[4] Psalm 80.1; Isaiah 63.9; 40.11
[5] Mark 2.18–20
[6] *see* Ephesians 5.22–33
[7] Revelation 19.7; 21.2
[8] Mark 12
[9] John 15

the wilderness to seek and to save even one lost sheep, laying down His life for His sheep, leading them out into good pasture and protecting them from the wolves.[1]

The four other principal metaphors of the Church in the Bible also illumine the relationship which God has established with His people, although they carry further implications as well.

First, God's people are a *kingdom*, the sphere of His rule, 'His dominion'.[2] The original Israelite theocracy, which was repudiated when the people asked for a king like the heathen nations, has been recovered and spiritualized through Christ. In saving us God 'has delivered us from the dominion of darkness and transferred us to the kingdom of his beloved Son'.[3] And Christ exercises His rule in His people through His Spirit, 'for the kingdom of God does not mean food and drink but righteousness and peace and joy in the Holy Spirit'.[4]

Next, God's people are His *household* or *family*. What was dimly adumbrated in the Old Testament, where Israel was named God's son,[5] is fully worked out in the New. In Christ God begets us again, makes us His children, adopts us into His family and sends His Spirit into our hearts that we may call Him 'Abba Father'.[6] Much of the Christian life is determined, as Jesus taught, by this intimate, filial relationship with God. We are to take no anxious thought even for the material necessities of life, because our Heavenly Father knows our needs. We are rather to occupy ourselves with Him, with His kingdom and His righteousness, to commit ourselves and our affairs to Him, to trust Him to take care of us, and all we need will be given us.[7]

Thirdly, God's people are a *building* 'not made with hands', a building which God is Himself constructing, the rebuilt spiritual temple, with Jesus Christ as the only foundation as witnessed to by apostles and prophets, and the Holy Spirit as the shekinah presence in the sanctuary.[8]

Fourthly, God's people are the *body of Christ*, the most

prominent image in Paul's letters and the only one with no Old Testament equivalent, with Christ as the Head to rule and nourish His body and the Holy Spirit as the breath to animate it.[9]

But each of these four pictures does more than illumine the relation between God and His people. It goes further and illustrates also the mutual relations and duties which God's people have. We are fellow-citizens of the kingdom, brothers and sisters in the family, living stones being built into the spiritual house, and above all members of Christ's body, not only receiving life and direction from the Head, but ourselves actively functioning and interdependent, and therefore forbidden either to despise or to envy one another.[10]

MANY METAPHORS – ONE MESSAGE

All this wealth of metaphor points in the same direction. In each image the stress is *either* on God's gracious initiative as Husband, Shepherd, King, Father, Builder, etc., *or* on His people as a redeemed community both in relation to Him as His bride, flock, family, body, etc., and in relation to each other as branches in the same vine, sheep in the same flock, children in the same family, members of the same body. No metaphor stands or falls by the inclusion of the clergy. This is simply not how the Bible thinks about the Church.

It is perfectly true that Paul likens himself to the best man at

[1] Luke 15.3–7; John 10
[2] Psalm 114.2
[3] Colossians 1.13
[4] Romans 14.17
[5] Hosea 11.1
[6] *for instance* 1 John 2.29–3.3; 3.9–10; Romans 8.14–17; Galatians 4.4–7
[7] Matthew 6.7–13, 25–34; 7.7–11
[8] 1 Corinthians 3.11, 16; Ephesians 2.20–22
[9] *for instance* Ephesians 4.4, 15–16; Colossians 2.19
[10] 1 Corinthians 12.14–26

the wedding, as did John the Baptist before him.[1] He also speaks of the teaching ministry of himself and Apollos in Corinth in terms of planting and watering the seed in God's field and of laying the foundation and erecting the super-structure of God's building.[2] Similarly, the ministers of the Church are described as under-shepherds to whom the care of the flock is entrusted,[3] as heralds of the kingdom, as stewards of the household, and even sometimes as nursemaids in the family.[4] It is true also that, although every Christian in the Church is a member of Christ's body with a function to perform, yet some organs appear to have a more important function than others, for instance the head than the feet and the eye than the hand,[5] although each needs the other and cannot dispense with it.

Nevertheless, every one of these details represents an appendix to the metaphor. The metaphor stands complete without them and, strictly speaking, is independent of them. They have a part to play, but it is a subsidiary part and, one might add, a dispensable part. A best man can be very useful at a wedding, but the bride and bridegroom can marry without one. Stewards and nursemaids are valuable in a home, but a father will not let his children starve for lack of them. No. The truths of central importance which all these church metaphors underline are God's gracious dealings with His people and their responsive duties to Him and to each other.

The essential unity of the Church, originating in the call of God and illustrated in the metaphors of Scripture, leads us to this conclusion: the responsibilities which God has entrusted to His Church He has entrusted to His *whole* Church. What are they? 'Once you were no people', Peter writes, 'but now you are God's people.' And God's people, he further explains, are both a *priestly* people, to offer to Him the acceptable, spiritual sacrifices of praise and prayer, and a *missionary* people, to declare to others the excellences of their God, the God who has called them into His marvellous light and has had mercy upon them.[6] In brief, God's people are intended to be a worshipping and witnessing community. And both these duties belong to the whole Church as the Church. The clergy cannot monopolize them; nor can the laity escape them. Neither clergy nor laity can delegate them to the other; there is no possibility of worship or witness by proxy.

To insist upon this is a healthy corrective to the exaggerated clericalism which has too often and too long kept the laity in subjection and condemned them to a position of inferiority and inactivity. Clericalism is due to a distorted image of the Church. Certainly, God calls clergy to an important work, but their position is always subordinate to that of the Church as a whole, God's own redeemed community. The laity will only find their rightful place in the Church when the simple truth is recognized, that the clergy are there to serve the Church, not the Church the clergy. In order to gain recognition for this truth, we must recover the biblical doctrine of the Church as the people of God, and in particular these truths – that in all matters of status and privilege God's people are by God's call one and undifferentiated, and that the offering of worship to God and the bearing of witness to the world are the inalienable right and duty of this one people, the whole Church, clergy and laity together.

[1] 2 Corinthians 11.2; John 3.29
[2] 1 Corinthians 3.5–15
[3] *for instance* Acts 20.28; 1 Peter 5.1–4
[4] *for instance* Acts 20.25; 1 Corinthians 4; 1 Thessalonians 2.7
[5] 1 Corinthians 12.21
[6] *see* 1 Peter 2.5, 9–10

2

The Christian Ministry *(diakonia)*

WE began with the Church, the whole people of God, because this is the preoccupation of Scripture. The story Scripture tells is the story of a people called by God to be distinct from other peoples, the story of this people's varied fortunes according to their varied reactions to the divine call. But everywhere the principal interest is in the people as a unity, and in the God who repeatedly says to them: 'I will be your God, and you shall be my people.' The distinctive character of every member of the Church of God is not something which may make him different from his fellow church members, but his very membership of Christ and of Christ's Church, which makes him different from the rest of mankind. And because God's people are different, 'holy', they are called to exhibit their difference in their behaviour. 'I am the Lord your God. You shall not do as they do in the land of Egypt, where you dwelt, and you shall not do as they do in the land of Canaan, to which I am bringing you. You shall not walk in their statutes. You shall do my ordinances and keep my statutes and walk in them. I am the Lord your God.'[1] Jesus said much the same thing to His disciples, the nucleus of the new Israel: 'You know that the rulers of the Gentiles lord it over them, and their great men exercise authority over them. It shall not be so among you.'[2] And the same divine call to be different, to be holy, is heard in the Epistles: 'you must no longer live as the Gentiles do'.[3]

This then is the basic difference of which God's people are aware. The differentiation is not in the Church, but from the world. They are one with each other but separate from the world because holy unto the Lord.

Nevertheless, within the undifferentiated unity of the people of God differences do exist – differences which relate not to their standing before God but to their function in the community.[4] This contrast between unity and diversity is drawn by the apostle Paul in his letters at least three times, and on each occasion he makes use of the analogy of a single human body consisting of many parts. For example,

> as in one body we have many members, and all the members do not have the same function, so we, though many, are one body in Christ, and individually members one of another. Having gifts that differ according to the grace given to us, let us use them.[5]

The most elaborate exposition of this combination of unity and diversity is in 1 Corinthians 12. The chapter begins with an emphatic declaration that all Christians share in the same Spirit. It is one and the same Spirit who has enabled us all to say 'Jesus is Lord' (verses 1–3). It is one and the same Spirit who has distributed to us different gifts (verses 4–11). And it is one and the same Spirit of whom we have drunk and with whom we have been baptized into one body (verses 12, 13). Nevertheless, this one body does not consist of one member but of many (verse 14), and he goes on to list some of the different spiritual gifts for service which the one Spirit has bestowed or (for it comes to the same thing) some of the different kinds of Christian work the one Spirit has 'appointed' (verse 28).

Some of these gifts or workers certainly do not exist in the Church today, notably apostles and prophets, the first two named. Probably some others like 'workers of miracles' have also ceased. But we can all agree that 'teachers' are still equipped with a teaching gift and appointed to serve in the Church. In Ephesians 4.11 they are linked with 'pastors', a

[1] Leviticus 18.2–4
[2] Matthew 20.25–26
[3] Ephesians 4.17
[4] 'Ministry and laity are one. There may be a difference in function but there is no difference in essence' (Report of the Committee on 'Progress in the Anglican Communion', *Lambeth Conference, 1958*, p. 2.113)
[5] Romans 12.4–6

word seeming to indicate the more settled pastoral ministry of the Church, and, as in the other passages already quoted, it is only 'some' who are appointed to serve in this way and given by Christ to His Church.

It is clear, therefore, that although the body is one to which we all belong, and although the Spirit is one of whom we have all partaken, so that we enjoy a common status and privilege, yet different members of the one body are appointed and equipped by the one Spirit to perform different functions. Some are 'pastors and teachers', or 'shepherds and teachers', whose particular calling is to tend and teach the rest of the flock. So the question before us now is: what is the relation between these two groups, between teachers and taught, shepherds and flock, or in modern, unbiblical terminology between 'clergy' and 'laity'? Four main answers have been given to this question. The first is 'clericalism'.

CLERICALISM

By 'clericalism', to which I have already referred, is meant the clerical domination of the laity. That this has been the commonest tendency appears from the fate suffered by the word 'lay'. Originally, the Greek word *laos* meant quite simply 'people', any people or crowd of people. In secular Greek it was used of the population of a city-state, and in biblical Greek of the people of God, first 'Israel' in contrast to the Gentiles[1] and then 'the new Israel' (the Church) including Gentiles.[2] Thus it was an inclusive word and indicated all the members of a certain people. However, the word had within it from the beginning the seeds of its own decay, for it was natural to continue using it of the masses even when it was desired to distinguish them from their leaders. The *laos* of a Greek city-state were thus distinguished from the *kleros*, the magistrate, and in the Gospels we read of 'the chief priests and the rulers and the people',[3] suggesting that the former were not part of the latter.

In the course of time the English word became even further debased, until in current parlance 'lay' is often a synonym for 'amateur' as opposed to 'professional', or 'unqualified' as opposed to 'expert'. Indeed, the term has developed a largely apologetic flavour when used of oneself ('I'm afraid I'm a layman in this field') and a derisory one when used of others ('he's only a layman, he doesn't speak with knowledge'). Hendrik Kraemer points out that a similar fate has befallen the Greek term *idiotes*, which originally meant the private individual or civilian as opposed to the official, or the ordinary person in contrast to the specialist. This is what the Sanhedrin perceived Peter and John to be, both 'uneducated' (*agrammatoi*) and 'common men' (*idiotai*).[4] But today, of course, the idiot is not the uncultured person, but the imbecile.

The devaluation of the word 'lay' is but a symptom of the devaluation of the people 'laity'. Several historical factors contributed to the process. Theologically, the identification of the Christian presbyter with the Old Testament priest and the representation of the Eucharist as the Christian sacrifice, first clearly enunciated by Cyprian Bishop of Carthage in the middle of the third century, carried with it the priest–people distinction which had existed indeed in the Old Testament but has been superseded in the New by the priesthood of all believers, that is, the priesthood of the whole Church. Practically, one suspects that disciplinary problems were a major cause of clericalism, since authoritarian measures were sometimes taken to subdue insubordinate laity. But the Christian presbyter is no more a New Testament apostle than he is an Old Testament priest, and the exercise of ecclesiastical discipline belongs to the whole

[1] *for instance* Acts 4.10 – literally 'all the people Israel'
[2] *for instance* Acts 15.14: 'God . . . visited the Gentiles, to take out of them a people for his name'
[3] Luke 23.13; *compare* 20.19
[4] Acts 4.13

congregation, not to its leaders only. See, for example, Our Lord's injunction, 'tell it to the church',[1] and the apostle's instructions to the Corinthian Church to take action as a body to excommunicate the incestuous offender: 'When you are assembled . . . you are to deliver this man to Satan. . . .' And again, 'Drive out the wicked person from among you'.[2]

However the suppression of the laity arose historically, there can be no doubt that clericalism still permeates much of our thinking today. Kraemer quotes the Roman Catholic author Yves Congar: 'lay people will always form a subordinate order in the church'.[3] And though the Church of England has never articulated the matter in such terms, it has often behaved as if it thought this way. Indeed, nearly everybody in England does think this way. People's unconscious identification of the Church with the clergy betrays itself in several popular expressions: 'he's going into the Church' for 'he is entering the ordained ministry' and 'why doesn't the Church do something?' for 'why doesn't the archbishop or the episcopate or convocation do something?'

Indeed, since I am myself a parson, I am obliged to ask which of us in the ordained ministry is entirely free from blame? It is true that some of the laity acquiesce too readily in our clericalism. That is to say, they plead that they have no time, or that they are untrained and prefer to leave things to the expert, or that they bear heavy responsibilities in the world and would prefer to be passive and docile and occupy a back seat in the Church. And with such pleas they hand over to the clergy obligations and privileges which are theirs by divine right as Christian people. In the words of Sir John Lawrence, editor of *Frontier*, 'what does the layman really want? He wants a building which looks like a church; a clergyman dressed in the way he approves; services of the kind he's been used to, *and to be left alone.*'[4]

So we parsons trade on their excuses and claim as our prerogative what belongs properly to the whole Church. Thank

God some of the more biblically orientated laity revolt. 'Too often our pastors seem to treat us only as fund raisers, or cooks, or mimeograph machine operators . . . when our hearts are crying out for a meaningful ministry.'[5] Sir Kenneth Grubb records what happened a century ago when Roman Catholic laity in England 'showed signs of being uppish'. 'They were well and truly sat on', he writes.

> Mgr George Talbot wrote as follows to Archbishop Manning in 1857, 'What is the province of the laity? To hunt, to shoot, to entertain. These matters they understand, but to meddle with ecclesiastical matters, they have no right at all!'[6]

The clerical mind not infrequently goes beyond this kind of condescension to actual tyranny. It manifests itself particularly in the composing of PCC agendas and the chairing of PCC meetings. It is perfectly possible to argue, and it is often argued, that certain subjects (like the conduct of public worship) are the parish clergyman's prerogative and have nothing to do with the laity. No doubt English church tradition, together with the provisions of the 1919 Enabling Act and of other subsequent legislation, give to PCCs only a limited jurisdiction. No doubt also some PCCs contain both unconverted and unspiritual members whose minds are not 'governed with the Spirit and Word of God'[7] and who therefore cannot be trusted to decide matters of great spiritual moment for the good of the parish. In some situations a Council may need to win its Chairman's trust by demonstrating its good sense and spirituality. But when God has blessed a vicar's ministry, and the elected Council are mature, responsible Christian men and women, and when a relationship of mutual respect and confidence has developed between minister and council, is there *any* matter affecting the

---

[1] Matthew 18.17
[2] 1 Corinthians 5.4–5, 13
[3] Kraemer: *A Theology of the Laity*, p. 11
[4] quoted in Robinson: *Layman's Church*, p. 10
[5] a quotation from the dustcover of Chafin: *Help! I'm a Layman*
[6] Grubb: *A Layman looks at the Church*, p. 26
[7] Article XXI, Book of Common Prayer, 1622

life, worship, work and witness of the church which should be excluded from the PCC agenda?[1] I can only speak from my own experience that our annual PCC day conferences, in which our priorities as a church have been discussed, including our public worship of God, our fellowship with one another and the church's whole evangelistic programme, have proved times of considerable profit and consequent advance. And with the arrival of synodical government it will become increasingly important for PCCs to debate diocesan and national as well as parochial issues.

Further, once items are put on the agenda, the vicar is bound to follow democratic procedures in the conduct of the Council's business. His duty is to help the Council to discover and clarify its common mind. The very idea of bulldozing the Council into letting him have his own way or even of attempting to exercise a chairman's veto should be abhorrent to him. Our own Council believe strongly in the Holy Spirit, and in His desire and ability to lead us in any matter to a common mind, the mind of Christ. We have therefore hardly, if ever, taken a vote. To foreclose an issue by a majority decision is usually a sign of impatient unbelief in the Holy Spirit; it can also sow seeds of further discord in the future. Of course several times a difference of opinion has arisen, but our policy has been to go on talking and praying together until we reach agreement rather than to act precipitately and force a division. I can think of two particular issues on which there was a sharp disagreement. The first concerned whether in St Peter's, Vere Street, our beautiful Georgian Chapel of Ease, we should rebuild the old pipe organ or install an electronic one. The second involved the use of modern English in public worship, especially whether God should be addressed as 'you'. Strong opinions were held on both sides. Opposing views were expressed and argued. The debate for many months was keen. For a while we wondered if we would ever reach agreement and whether it would not be essential to decide by voting. But we sought to be patient, to understand one another and to pray, and in the end the decisions made were, I think, unanimous.

I confess, however, that I personally do not always find these slow, democratic, Christian processes congenial. When an issue becomes tangled, one is tempted to lose patience and cut the Gordian knot. But autocratic clericalism is destructive of the Church, defiant to the Holy Spirit and disobedient to Christ. Christ's own teaching on the subject is unmistakable:

> 'You know that those who are supposed to rule over the Gentiles lord it over them, and their great men exercise authority over them. But it shall not be so among you; but whoever would be great among you must be your servant (*diakonos*), and whoever would be first among you must be slave (*doulos*) of all.'[2]

The contrast is complete. Heathen leadership is characterized by lordship and authority, Christian leadership by service, even slavery. As Hendrik Kraemer neatly puts it, 'the lust for power and dominion is exchanged for lust for *diakonia*'.[3] And in this as in all things Jesus is our perfect model. He 'emptied himself, taking the form of a servant (*doulos*)'.[4] Though His disciples' lord (*kurios*) and teacher, He put on a servant's apron and performed a servant's job in washing their feet.[5] Indeed, He said to them in the same upper room 'I am among you as one who serves' (*ho diakonon*).[6] He added: 'If I then, your Lord and Teacher, have washed your feet, you also ought to wash one another's feet. For I have given you an example, that you also should do as I have done to you'[7]. As Michael Green has expressed it in his forthright book *Called to Serve*: 'Jesus is *the* Servant... The Church must be the Church of the Servant.'[8]

The choice between lordship and servitude still confronts

---

[1] Resolution 24 of the 1968 Lambeth Conference reads: 'The Conference recommends that no major issue in the life of the Church should be decided without the full participation of the laity in discussion and in decision.' For lack of this full participation of laity in their own conference the bishops admit that their report is not 'the balanced document' they would have wished (p. 120).

[2] Mark 10.42–44   [3] Kraemer: *A Theology of the Laity*, p. 146
[4] Philippians 2.7   [5] John 13.3–15
[6] Luke 22.24–27   [7] John 13.14–15
[8] Green: *Called To Serve*, p. 14

every man called to the ministry of the Church. The apostles themselves were conscious of it. 'Not that we lord it over your faith', wrote Paul; 'we work with you for your joy'. 'Not as domineering over those in your charge', wrote Peter, 'but being examples to the flock.'[1] Not lords but servants, not bosses, but fellow-workers and examples.

ANTICLERICALISM

The second possible relation between clergy and laity is the exact opposite of the one we have so far been considering. I called the first 'clericalism'; I will call the second 'anticlericalism'. The spirit of clericalism is to despise the laity, and behave as if they did not exist. The spirit of anticlericalism is to despise the clergy and to behave as if they did not exist, or rather, since they do exist, to wish they didn't.

Anticlericalism is a natural and understandably vigorous reaction to clericalism. Historically, it was current clerical abuses which led both Quakers and Christian Brethren to dispense with an ordained ministry altogether, although both preserve some kind of 'oversight', corporately exercised over the local meeting or assembly by its acknowledged leaders.

Before going any further, it is important for us to notice that there are traces of a real anticlericalism in the New Testament itself, not because the church leaders were abusing their authority, but because their followers were exhibiting an altogether exaggerated deference towards them. It is this unseemly personality cult which lies behind the slogans recorded in I Corinthians 1.12 'I am of Paul, and I of Apollos'. Paul is so horrified by this exhibition of allegiance to men instead of to Christ, as if Paul were their crucified Saviour and they had been baptized into the name of Paul, that he cries out with indignant sarcasm: '*What* then is Apollos? *What* is Paul?'[2] He uses the neuter, 'what', deliberately, as if he is asking: 'What on earth do you suppose we are that you pay this ridiculous homage to us?' And then he answers his own question, almost denigrating his office: We're just *diakonoi*, he says, waiters at table, whom God has been pleased to use. Again, we are nothing but Christ's 'underlings' and the stewards of God's revelation,[2] and *that's* how people should regard us.

In this latter half of the twentieth century a new form of anticlericalism is abroad. It is a reaction not to abuse but to redundancy. Since the process of urbanization has (in city areas) made the parochial system (to say the least) artificial, the welfare state has taken over much of the community care previously exercised by clergy, and the distressed often turn for help to a psychiatrist rather than a pastor, many people are wondering what clergy are now for and whether they are needed any longer. One might call this rather a spirit of a-clericalism than of anticlericalism. It must be honestly faced. Is there any room left for clergy? Might not the laity take over?

If we seek an answer to these questions in the right place, namely in the New Testament, I think we must conclude that a pastoral ministry of some kind is part of Christ's permanent purpose for His Church (although it may take different forms – stipendiary and voluntary, full-time and part-time, settled and itinerant), and that we have no authority to abolish it.

Whatever view we may hold of the status of the apostles and the question of their successors, it is clear that the Twelve were appointed by Jesus Himself and trained for a special ministry. It is also clear that the Twelve arranged for the appointment of the seven to relieve them of social administration and free them to concentrate on prayer and preaching. Both these groups, however, were in some respects unique. It is when we come to the missionary journeys of Paul that a regular pattern begins to emerge. It is extremely significant that, on revisiting the Galatian cities of Lystra, Iconium and Antioch, Paul and Barnabas 'appointed elders for them in every church, with

[1] 2 Corinthians 1.24; 1 Peter 5.3
[2] 1 Corinthians 3.5
[3] 1 Corinthians 4.1

prayer and fasting.'[1] This became Paul's consistent practice. There is no mention in the Acts record of the appointment of elders (presbyter-bishops) in Philippi, but Paul refers to them and to the deacons in his Philippian letter.[2] Again, Luke does not mention in Acts the appointment of elders in Ephesus, but Paul sends for them to Miletus and addresses to them the memorable speech recorded in Acts 20. And when we reach the Pastoral Epistles the same pattern is being continued. 'This is why I left you in Crete,' Paul writes to Titus, 'that you might amend what was defective, and appoint elders in every town as I directed you.'[3] Indeed, whatever arrangements were made on the human level for the selection, appointment and ordination of the pastors of Christ's flock, the apostle declares that fundamentally they are Christ's gift to His Church.[4]

We must go further than this and say that the elders occupied a real position of leadership in the local church. Two principal verbs are used to denote the character of this leadership. The first is *proïstemi*. 'We beseech you, brethren, to respect those who labour among you and *are over you* in the Lord and admonish you, and to esteem them very highly in love because of their work.'[5] In 1 Timothy 3.5 it is asked how a man who 'does not know how to manage his own household' can possibly 'care for God's Church'. Here *proïstemi* is used for the man's management of his own family, but is changed when it comes to the care of God's. In 1 Timothy 5.17, however, certain elders are specified as being 'worthy of double honour', namely those 'who rule well', where the verb is *proïstemi* again.

According to the Arndt–Gingrich Lexicon *proïstemi* has two meanings, first to 'be at the head of, rule, direct' and secondly to 'be concerned about, care for, give aid'. It is undoubtedly used in this latter sense in Romans 12.8 ('he who gives aid') and in a similar way in Titus 3.8, 14, of people who 'apply themselves to' or 'busy themselves with' good works. But it seems to describe 'headship' or 'oversight' in reference to the potential presbyters' and deacons' management of their households.[6]

Probably, therefore, a similar authority, but over God's household, is intended in both 1 Thessalonians 5.12 and 1 Timothy 5.17. We must observe, however, that the elder's leadership is exercised by 'labouring' among the people, and that this 'labour' is specified in 1 Timothy 5.17 as being 'in preaching and teaching'.[7]

The second verb used for clerical leadership is *hegeomai*. It occurs three times in Hebrews 13, translated 'your leaders'.[8] The same word is used of Joseph when he was '*governor* over Egypt and over all his (Pharaoh's) household'[9] and even of Christ in the quotation from Micah's prophecy: 'from you (*sc.* Bethlehem) shall come *a ruler* who will govern (*literally*, 'shepherd') my people Israel'.[10] Since this is the word used in Hebrews 13 of local Christian leaders, presumably presbyters, we cannot deny that the minister exercises some kind of 'rule'. But we must be very careful how we understand it. Luke put the word into the mouth of Jesus Himself when He said: 'let the greatest among you become as the youngest, and the leader as one who serves.'[11] So then, although Jesus recognizes that there will and must be 'leadership' in the Christian Church, He interprets it in terms of service, and the context of Hebrews 13 shows what form this leadership service will take. Christian leaders are to be given both 'obedience' and 'submission', the author writes, 'for they are keeping watch over your souls, as men who will have to give account'.[12] Again, it is they who 'spoke to you the word of God', whose faith is to be imitated.[13]

[1] Acts 14.23
[2] Philippians 1.1
[3] Titus 1.5
[4] Ephesians 4.11
[5] 1 Thessalonians 5.12–13
[6] 1 Timothy 3.5, 12
[7] the verb is *kopiao* in both verses, meaning 'to toil'
[8] this is the plural participle *hoi hegoumenoi humon* in Hebrews 13.7, 17, 24; *compare* Acts 15.22, where the expression is used of Judas Barsabbas and Silas
[9] Acts 7.10
[10] Matthew 2.6
[11] Luke 22.26: '*ho hegoumenos hos ho diakonon*'
[12] Hebrews 13.17; 1 Corinthians 16.16
[13] Hebrews 13.7

Summarizing this evidence, no biblical Christian can give in to the extreme anticlericalism which wants either to dispense with a ministry altogether or deny it any authority. No Christ and His apostles intended the Church to have a pastoral elder-ship or 'oversight'.[1] Such oversight involves some kind of 'direction' or 'rule'. But it is to be seen as a form of service and is to be exercised in general through watching over men's souls and in particular through the teaching of God's Word and through example. We must beware of the spirit of Diotrephes who liked to put himself first.[2] We are called to oversight not lordship, to a leadership which leads not by coercion but by the authority of instruction and example.

DUALISM

If we avoid the extremes of clericalism and of anticlericalism, of a domineering ministry on the one hand and a dispensable one on the other, does this suggest that we should settle for a dualistic compromise? That is, are we to hold that clergy and laity have both received a divine vocation, though a different one, that each party has its own sphere, that we must delineate their territories carefully and avoid all trespass? This is the third possible relation between clergy and laity.

I think it is still the Roman Catholic view. It probably began with the Old Testament analogy of the distinction between priest and people in which the people were forbidden to enter the temple or to sacrifice, while various practices were forbidden to the priests because they had been consecrated to the Lord. However the distinction arose, it is certain that the spread of monasticism hardened it, with its disastrous severance of the sacred from the secular, the Church from the world. 'Duo sunt genera Christianorum', wrote Gratian, the twelfth-century lawyer. 'There are two sorts of Christians.' And Canon Law of the Church of Rome went into elaborate details to define and distinguish the *status clericalis* and the *status laïcalis*.

38

In *The Documents of Vatican II* there is certainly a welcome new emphasis on the importance of the laity. Introducing the Decree on the Apostolate of the Laity, Martin H. Work quotes the pungent comment of one layman:

> The lay apostolate has been simmering on the 'back burner' of the Church's apostolic life for nearly two thousand years, and finally the Fathers of this Council moved it up to the 'front burner' and turned the heat up all the way.

Martin Work adds how 'everyone hopes it will "come to a boil" soon. . .'[3] In the first major document of the Council, *Lumen Gentium*, the Dogmatic Constitution on the Church, clear statements of the equal dignity of clergy and laity appear. For example 'all (in the Church) share a true equality with regard to the dignity and to the activity common to all the faithful for the building up of the Body of Christ'.[4] Again, 'let sacred pastors recognize and promote the dignity as well as the responsibility of the layman in the Church'.[5] These are heartening sentiments.

Yet in the same document there are prominent traces of the older view. In *Mystici Corporis Christi*, the papal encyclical of 1943, it had been stated that bishops are the 'primary and principal' element in the constitution of the Church. And Vatican II endorsed this: 'In the bishops . . . our Lord Jesus Christ . . . is present in the midst of those who believe.'[6] So apparently it is still by *bishops* that the Church is constituted and the presence of Christ mediated. The order of the early chapters of the Dogmatic Constitution on the Church is significant in this respect. The opening two chapters are entitled 'The Mystery of the Church' and 'the People of God'. But then comes 'the Hierarchical Structure of the Church,

[1] Acts 20.28; 1 Peter 5.2
[2] 3 John 9
[3] *The Documents of Vatican II*, p. 486
[4] *The Documents of Vatican II*, p. 58
[5] *The Documents of Vatican II*, p. 64
[6] *The Documents of Vatican II*, p. 40

with special reference to the Episcopate', while 'the Laity' is chapter 4. This chapter begins: 'Having set forth the functions of the hierarchy, this holy Synod gladly turns its attention to the status of those faithful called the laity.'[1] They are evidently still second-class citizens after all. They do not themselves constitute the Church; it is just that 'their sacred pastors know how much the laity contribute to the welfare of the entire Church'.[2] The verbs to 'constitute' (of bishops and their assistants the priests) and to 'contribute' (of laity) are revealing of the old dualism.

The Orthodox view is similar to the Roman, but less dualistic. Hendrik Kraemer expresses it by the quotation 'clergy and laity make together the fulness (*pleroma*) of the church'.[3] However, in contrast to the Church of Rome, the Eastern Orthodox Churches have 'a far livelier, more immediate awareness of the wholeness of the Church as the redeemed community in which all are active participants'.[4]

What about the Church of England? By contrast with Vatican II's Dogmatic Constitution on the Church mentioned above, it is very welcome to see that Lambeth 1968's Report on 'Renewal in Ministry' adopts the opposite order. It begins with 'Laymen and Laywomen', continues with the ordained ministry and ends with the episcopate. Yet in the Church of England I would say that a fairly rigid dualism, although not always theologically defined, is nevertheless generally accepted. The parson has his job and the layman his. They are different and should be kept apart. Neither should invade the other's domain. This is a kind of comity arrangement, and comity can easily degenerate into rivalry. At its worst it breeds a 'hands off my preserve' attitude, especially in the mind of the clergyman – a mentality which assigns to the laity a lesser and lower role and is therefore but a thinly disguised version of the clericalism we have rejected. At its best, a real partnership can develop, which is infinitely better than either clericalism or anticlericalism, in which parson and people respect each other's dominions and co-exist in happy harmony. It is for partner-

40

ship' that George Goyder makes his impassioned plea in his *The People's Church.*

But we still have to investigate this dualism and ask where its ground and justification are to be found. It cannot be defended from the New Testament. *Kleros* and *laos* were distinguished as magistrate and people in the Greek city-states, but in the New Testament 'they denote the same people, not different people'.[5]

Again, we must insist that the distinction between priests and people, so familiar in the Old Testament, each group with its own duties and rights, is not perpetuated in the New. The word *hiereus* is employed in the New Testament only of three people – of Old Testament priests, of Jesus Christ 'a great priest over the house of God',[6] who sacrificed Himself once on the cross and ever lives to intercede for us, and of all Christian people whom Christ has made 'priests to his God and Father'[7] and who together constitute the priesthood which continuously offers up the spiritual sacrifices of praise and thanksgiving, acceptable to God through Jesus Christ.[8] It is indeed a well-known fact that the word is never used of the Christian minister, who is a presbyter, but not a priest.

So we must ask: if the New Testament does not distinguish between *kleros* and *laos*, or between priest and people, but only between the congregation and its leaders, what function is there which a minister may perform and a layman may not? After all, in the Church of England a layman may lead services of worship, and preach if he becomes a licensed Reader. And any layman may baptize in an emergency, so that the validity of baptism does not depend on the baptizer. A lay Reader may also administer the cup at Holy Communion, with special permission. What *biblical* reason can be adduced for allowing

[1] *The Documents of Vatican II*, p. 56   [2] *The Documents of Vatican II*, p. 57
[3] *The Documents of Vatican II*, p. 96   [4] Bliss: *We the People*, p. 87
[5] W. Robinson: *Completing The Reformation, The Doctrine of The Priesthood Of All Believers* (Lexington, Kentucky, College of the Bible, 1955)
[6] Hebrews 10.21
[7] Revelation 1.6; 5.10; 20.6
[8] 1 Peter 2.5

him to administer in one kind but not in the other? H. Kraemer describes what happened to the Evangelical (that is the Lutheran) Church in Silesia, 198 of whose 200 pastors were evacuated when Silesia became Polish.

> The laymen took over the care of the Church completely. The Sunday services, including preaching, the administration of the Sacraments, religious instruction for adults and young people, pastoral care in all its forms, were looked after by the laity.[1]

And why not?[2] In that emergency, it was the only solution. We must therefore challenge the dualism which explains the relations between clergy and laity in terms of departmentalization. *Of course* we should largely restrict the administration of Word and Sacraments to the clergy. As Article XXIII puts it: 'it is not lawful for any man to take upon him the office of publick preaching, or ministering the sacraments in the congregation, before he be lawfully called, and sent to execute the same.'[3] But we must be clear that this is a question of *order* not of *doctrine*. It does not in itself supply a satisfactory biblical basis for clergy–laity relations.

SERVICE

Clergy are not to domineer over the laity (clericalism), nor to denigrate themselves and pretend they are altogether dispensable (anticlericalism), nor jealously to defend their preserves against trespass, while allocating other preserves to the laity (dualism), but to recognize that the laity are the Church and that they, the clergy, are appointed to serve them, to seek to equip them to be what God intends them to be. This is the fourth and the proper relation between clergy and laity.

We have already seen that we are called to serve, not to rule. We are servants of Christ, His 'underlings' or 'errand-boys'.[4] We are also the servants of others for Christ's sake.[5] And though this is true of every disciple of Christ, it is especially true of those called to positions of leadership in the Church: 'let . . .

42

the leader (become) as one who serves'.[6] At the beginning of June 1967 the Bishop of Winchester spoke to his Diocesan Conference about the Fenton Morley report. He told them of a saying current in the Roman Catholic Church since the Vatican Council: 'the bishops are the servants of the clergy, the clergy are the servants of the laity, the laity are kings with a servant problem'. It would not be difficult thus to caricature the call of clergy to serve the laity; we must try to understand how God means it to work out.

The apostle Peter in his first epistle takes from Exodus 19.4–6 the epithets with which God through Moses designated the Israelite people, and transfers them to the new Israel, the Christian Church. By so doing he indicates not only who God's people are but what their chief duties and functions are. First, they are 'a holy priesthood, to offer spiritual sacrifices acceptable to God through Jesus Christ'. It is often said nowadays that the Church exists for the world. This is an unbalanced half-truth. First and foremost the Church exists for God. He has called this people out of the world to be His special people,[7] 'a people for his name',[8] that they may give to Him the glory which is due to His name. So the first duty of the Church is worship, and the first service of the clergy to the laity should be to help them to worship, to teach them how to worship, to lead them in their worship (though not invariably).

Secondly, Peter wrote:

you are a chosen race, a royal priesthood, a holy nation, God's own

[1] Kraemer: *A Theology of the Laity*, p. 34

[2] For Anglican teaching on laymen as ministers of Word and Sacrament from the Reformation to 1662, *see* R. T. Beckwith: *Priesthood and Sacraments* (Marcham, 1964), p. 42–46; for Bishop J. A. T. Robinson's outspoken criticism of what he calls 'the clergy line' and the false 'mystique' or 'semi-magical status' often attributed to clergy, *see The New Reformation?*, p. 56–57

[3] Book of Common Prayer, 1662

[4] 'Errand-boys' is a popular version of *diakonoi* which I once heard used by Canon Leon Morris, Principal of Ridley College, Melbourne

[5] 2 Corinthians 4.5

[6] Luke 22.26

[7] Titus 2.14; *compare* 1 Peter 2.9: *laos periousios*

[8] Acts 15.14

people, that you may declare the wonderful deeds of him who called you out of darkness into his marvellous light.[1]

If the Church's first duty is Godward (worship), its second is manward (witness). More generally, the Church is called to ministry. It is a body with many limbs and organs, and each has a service to perform. 'There are varieties of service, but the same Lord.'[2] This service is *diakonia*, 'ministry'. So Christian ministry is not and cannot be restricted to the ordained ministry. Kenneth Chafin quotes Francis O. Ayres in *The Ministry of the Laity* (Westminster, 1962):

> if you are a baptized Christian, you are already a minister. Whether you are ordained or not is immaterial. No matter how you react, the statement remains true. You may be surprised, alarmed, pleased, antagonized, suspicious, acquiescent, scornful or enraged. Nevertheless, you are a minister of Christ.[3]

And the greatest ministry to which the laity are called is witness to Jesus Christ, evangelism, which means spreading the good news about Him. Indeed, in many respects the laity are in a position to engage in this work far more effectively than the clergy, because 'the laity is the dispersion of the church',[4] 'immersed in the world',[5] penetrating more deeply into secular society than the average clergyman will ever get. So it is the clergy's job, so far as we are able, 'to minister to the laity as a whole in such a way that it can fulfil its destiny and live as *a Christian laity* in the world of today'.[6] Or, in Sir Kenneth Grubb's words,

> the layman's job is to be a pioneer . . . The layman, by the mere fact of living in the world, at his job, in his suburb, on travels for his firm, in his union, at his club, is in a pioneer rôle . . . As a pioneer in the world the layman can do much to interpret to the clergyman what it is all about.[7]

And, one might add, as a pastor, the clergyman is to help the layman to live for Christ and witness to Christ in his secular situation. Some suggestions how we may do this I shall reserve for the next chapter.

At this stage what we need to clarify is this relation of clergy to laity, the clergy serving, or one might even say 'servicing', the laity. Clear biblical warrant for this privileged relationship is supplied by Ephesians 4.11–12:

> And his gifts were that some should be apostles, some prophets, some evangelists, some pastors and teachers, for the equipment of the saints, for the work of ministry, for building up the body of Christ.

If we erase the comma after the word 'saints' and punctuate these verses as Armitage Robinson and others have argued, followed by NEB, we learn why Christ 'gave gifts to men', blessing His Church with pastors and teachers. The ultimate reason was 'for building up the body of Christ'. But how is this to be achieved? Only when pastors and teachers fulfil their calling, which is to 'equip the saints for the work of ministry'. The 'saints' are the laity, all the people of God. Their calling is to engage in 'the work of ministry', serving men in the world for Christ's sake. And the calling of the clergy is to 'equip' the saints to do it.

How the clergy are to perform this equipping work is suggested in the combination 'pastors and teachers'. Christian ministers are pastors, shepherds of Christ's flock. This is their only essential distinctness. Of course they are themselves also Christ's sheep. But they are called to be shepherds. The Church is a universal priesthood; and also a universal diaconate, for all God's people are called to *diakonia*. But the Church is not a universal pastorate. All God's people are priests; all are ministers or servants; but 'He gave *some* . . . pastors and teachers'.

The chief function of the pastor is teaching, for the chief duty of the shepherd is to feed or pasture his sheep. The ordained ministry is fundamentally a teaching ministry. This is why the

[1] 1 Peter 2.9   [2] 1 Corinthians 12.5
[3] Chafin: *Help! I'm a Layman*, p. 25
[4] Kraemer: *A Theology of the Laity*, p. 181
[5] J. A. T. Robinson: *Layman's Church*, p. 18; in *The New Reformation?* he writes of 'almost total immersion' in the world (p. 69)
[6] Kraemer: *A Theology of the Laity*, p. 174
[7] Grubb: *A Layman looks at the Church*, p. 30–31, 34

ordination candidate must be 'apt to teach'[1] and must also 'hold firm to the sure word as taught, so that he may be able to give instruction in sound doctrine and also to confute those who contradict it'.[2]

But, it may be objected, if the relation between clergy and laity is that of shepherd to sheep, of the teacher to the taught, are we not back where we started? Are we not guilty of encouraging lay passivity, even inertia (the clergy being the leaders) and lay ignorance (the clergy being the teachers)? Certainly there is an element here we cannot escape. At the same time, we repudiate both lordship and paternalism. And if it be said that the pastoral relationship makes the clergyman a subject and the layman an object, we must immediately add that it is only in order to help the layman to become himself a subject. The great purpose of the teaching ministry is not to tie our pupils to our apron-strings, but rather to help to lead them into spiritual maturity and active ministry.

There must be many of us in the Church, both clergy and laity, who need to perform a complete mental somersault. It is not the clergyman who is the really important person and the layman a rather inferior brand of churchman, but the other way round. It is the laity who are important, the whole Church serving both God and man, the vanguard of Christ's army as it advances to the conquest of the world, and the clergy are the servicing organization.[3]

We must once for all give up defining the laity in relation to and in distinction from the clergy. Yet this is the usual procedure. 'Who are the laity?' The *Oxford Dictionary* answer is 'the body of the people not in orders, as opposed to the clergy'. The *Oxford Dictionary of the Christian Church* is no better. It defines 'Laity' as 'Members of the Christian Churches who do not belong to the clergy'. Dr Kathleen Bliss expresses a trenchant criticism of all such negative attitudes to and definitions of the laity. For these, she writes, 'have in them a strong element of "over-againstness" towards the clergy – the clergy are, and the laity are not; the clergy do, and the laity must not. Nobody wants to be an "is-not". . . '⁴ Instead, we must start defining the clergy in relation to the laity. The laity are the whole people of God, purchased by His precious blood, and some of us are given the great privilege of their oversight, shepherding and serving them for Christ's sake. The common phrase 'clergy and laity' is essentially dualistic. Clergy are not hyphenated to the laity as if they were a separate class; they are 'ministers *of* the people' because they themselves belong to the people they are called to serve.

I cannot conclude this chapter better than with something Paul wrote to the Corinthians. They were saying 'I belong to Paul', 'I belong to Apollos', or 'I belong to Cephas'. In other words, they were defining themselves in relation to their leaders. Paul told them that the opposite was the truth. 'All things are yours, whether Paul or Apollos or Cephas . . . all are yours.'⁵ So if anybody belongs to anybody in the Church, it is not the laity who belong to the clergy, but the clergy who belong to the laity. We are theirs, their servants for Jesus' sake. It is, therefore, when writing to a *layman* rather than to a *bishop* that we should sign our letters 'I have the honour to be, sir, your obedient servant'!

---

¹ I Timothy 3.2; *compare* 2 Timothy 2.24
² Titus 1.9
³ As the Swiss ecumenical leader Hans-Ruedi Weber has expressed it: 'The laity are not helpers of the clergy so that the clergy can do their job, but the clergy are helpers of the whole people of God, so that the laity can be the Church.' This is quoted by Robinson both in *Layman's Church* (p. 17) and in *The New Reformation?* (p. 55). He also quotes from Gibson Winter: *The New Creation as Metropolis*: 'the ministry is usually conceived today as the work of clergymen with auxiliary aids among the laity; ministry in the servant Church is the work of laity in the world with auxiliary help from theological specialists' (*The New Reformation?*, p. 65)
⁴ Bliss: *We The People*, p. 69
⁵ I Corinthians 3.21–22

3

The Christian Testimony *(marturia)*

In the last chapter I suggested that the whole Church is in a sense a 'diaconate' because it is called to *diakonia*, to service. 'I am among you as one who serves,' Jesus said,[1] and gave a visual demonstration of His words by girding Himself with a servant's apron and washing His disciples' feet. Then, when He had resumed His place at supper, He said to them:

> if I . . . your Lord and Teacher, have washed your feet, you also ought to wash one another's feet. For I have given you an example, that you also should do as I have done to you. Truly, truly, I say to you, a servant is not greater than his master.[2]

So every Christian is called to service.

But *diakonia* is a general word; there are many forms of service. As Dr Gustaf Wingren, Professor of Systematic Theology at the University of Lund in Sweden has written in his theological study of preaching and the Church:[3]

> Ordination of a Lutheran priest implies that in a Church where all are essentially priests, a household of God, he receives the special *task* of preaching the Word and dispensing the sacraments. The particular office which the priest holds is for Lutheranism but a special case of a general sharing out of vocations. The ministry of the priest is no *more* a ministry than is that of the mother or the doctor; it is simply that he has a *different* ministry from theirs, a totally different . . . The word 'ministry' is a word without content until it is known *what* ministry is in mind. Indeed, the practice of going around talking about 'the ministry' as something definite is an objectionable usage for a Lutheran priesthood, and implies in itself a false cleavage between the congregation and the priest, however modestly it may be done.

Acts 6 supplies a good example of the varied usage of *diakonia* in the New Testament. We are familiar with the appointment of the seven by the twelve. The apostles said 'it is not right that we should give up preaching the word of God to serve tables' (verse 2). But it is important to notice that both 'the ministry of the word' (verse 4) and the serving of tables (verse 2) are alluded to as forms of *diakonia*. Some would no doubt regard the one ministry as spiritual and the other as social, but both were 'service' and both required spiritual men to perform it.

The opportunities for *diakonia*, for a ministry in which Christian people may serve both God and man, are extremely numerous. There is the vocation of parents, especially of the mother, to bring up the children 'in the discipline and instruction of the Lord'[4] and to make the Christian home a place of love, hospitality and peace. There is a Christian's job, to be regarded primarily neither as a way to earn his living nor as a contribution to his country's economic stability, nor as a useful sphere of witness and evangelism – not in fact as a means to these or any other estimable ends – but as an end in itself, the *diakonia* of a Christian man, who is seeking to co-operate with the purpose of God in securing the welfare of men. There are also abundant openings for alert Christians in public service, through voluntary organizations, and among underprivileged and unwanted people in the neighbourhood.

But apart from the home, the job and the neighbourhood, most Christians will wish to be of service also in and through the local church to which they belong. It is fashionable nowadays, at least among more radical writers, to deride the notion of 'church service' as a regrettable kind of ecclesiastical self-centredness, and to insist that the proper sphere of a Christian's service is not the Church but the world. I do not deny the truth contained in this assertion. No Christian should live out his entire spare-time life in the sheltered seclusion of the church; he has been sent by his Master into the world, there

1 Luke 22.27
2 John 13.14–16
3 Gustaf Wingren: *The Living Word* (Sweden, 1949; English edition, scm Press, 1960), p. 104
4 Ephesians 6.4

49

to serve others humbly in His name. Yet we must not become unbalanced in applying this principle, either by denying that some church service is rightly church-centred or by asserting that it is all of this kind. Let me enlarge on these two points.

First, if a local church is to fulfil its God-given obligations of worship and fellowship, innumerable practical tasks have to be done. They are usually and rightly shared out among church members. I have in mind such good works as flower arrangement, clerical assistance, hospitality and catering, cleaning the church, mending the books, repairing the robes and maintaining the fabric. To these essential jobs we have ourselves in London added a creche for babies on Sunday mornings, the entertainment of visitors to lunch or coffee after Sunday services, and church guides who show visitors round on Sunday afternoons. These tasks are good and necessary; they should not be despised.

In the second place, however, it is a mistake to imagine that 'church service' is limited to this kind of church-centred activity. The service of the local church should include its evangelistic outreach to the parish or district in which the church building is situated. Each worshipping community should be a witness-ing community as well, and should be witnessing in the very neighbourhood in which it gathers for worship. There is some-thing very anomalous about a congregation which claims to be worshipping God, yet ignores the local residents who do not worship Him also. So one of the major aspects of true 'church service' will be the church's witness in its own district. Such service is not church-centred, since its concern is the secular world outside, but it will be church-based. The church is not the sphere in which it is performed, but the base of operations from which it is carried out.

This second aspect of church service also has many sections, which I will describe later, but they all have this in common: they all involve the opening of the mouth in *marturia*, in spoken testimony to people. For the Christian Church is a testifying

Church, and every Christian is called to be a witness. Possibly the last words which fell from the lips of the risen Christ before His ascension contained His command to be witnesses and His promise of the coming Spirit:

> you shall receive power when the Holy Spirit has come upon you; and you shall be my witnesses in Jerusalem and in all Judea and Samaria and to the end of the earth.[1]

We have no authority to separate the promise and the command from each other. If the gift of the Spirit belongs to all believers, the duty of witness belongs to all believers also.

Further, Christians need teaching and training for witness. Some would deny this. But those who do so probably have an unbalanced notion of witness, as if it meant merely the sharing of one's personal experience. The word 'witness' is not a synonym for autobiography, however; it means essentially testimony to Christ. 'You shall be *my* witnesses', He said. Again, 'the Spirit of truth . . . will bear witness *to me*; and you also are witnesses'.[2] And although witness to Christ may and should be illustrated and confirmed from our own experience, it is still about Christ that the true witness speaks, rather than about himself. But if he is to speak about Christ, he must know about Christ – not just the Christ of his own experience, but the Christ of the apostolic testimony. For the Christ about whom he must speak is the authentic Christ of the New Testament, whose birth, life, death, resurrection, heavenly reign and coming glory the apostles set forth in the New Testament documents.

And it is with this teaching and training of the laity to witness, as we began to suggest in the last chapter, that ordained ministers are particularly concerned. The laity have their *diakonia* (service), and especially their *marturia* (witness); the *diakonia* of the clergy is to help them to exercise it. Thus the humblest minister may borrow the customary designation of the Pope and style himself *servus servorum Dei*.

[1] Acts 1.8
[2] John 15.26–27

Dr Elton Trueblood, a prominent American Quaker, raises in his latest book the whole question of the purpose and function of the ordained ministry. He knows that many clergy are feeling frustrated and are uncertain of their function. They are sick and tired of appearing to exist merely in order to say an official prayer at functions or grace before banquets, and of being involved in endless promotional activity. As a result, many American clergy are leaving the ministry. Dr Trueblood says he knows of one insurance company which 'now employs more than a hundred former pastors'.[1] It is essential, therefore, to discover what a clergyman's distinctive ministry is. Dr Trueblood describes it as an 'equipping ministry'. He adds that he borrows the phrase from others,[2] although they in their turn derive the word from the RSV rendering of Ephesians 4.11–12: Christ's 'gifts were that some should be . . . pastors and teachers, for the *equipment* of the saints for the work of ministry'. Dr Trueblood goes on to write of the vital importance of training the laity: 'To watch for underdeveloped powers, to draw them out, to bring potency to actuality in human lives – this is a self-validating task.'[3]

If this work is fundamental to the duties of a clergyman, Dr Trueblood asks what we should call him. He is certainly a 'minister', but so is a layman. To call him an 'elder', he suggests, is rather absurd if he is a young man, as is 'father' if he is a bachelor. 'Preacher' refers to only one aspect of his ministry and 'pastor', though true and biblical, is somewhat misleading. 'Sheep are not particularly productive, except in providing wool and mutton',[4] and are also 'notorious for their placidity'. Besides, many town-dwellers have never even seen a sheep!

So Dr Trueblood settles for the word 'coach'.

Everyone knows that, in the development of a football or a baseball team, the quality of the coaching staff often makes a crucial difference . . . The glory of the coach is that of being the discoverer, the developer and the trainer of the powers of other men . . . The Christian coach will be one who is more concerned . . . in developing others than in enhancing his own prestige.[5]

Keith Miller, an episcopal layman from Corpus Christi, Texas, who has studied under Dr Trueblood, takes up this theme in *The Taste of New Wine*. He also refers to the clergyman as an 'equipping minister' or 'resource person', and adds that new church structures 'call for a kind of dying of our ecclesiastical ego'. No longer can the minister occupy the centre of the stage with 'God in the wings and the congregation as paying spectators'. Rather must the congregation hold the stage, in their homes and communities, with 'the minister in the wings and God the author of the drama as the audience'. He goes on:

the parish minister must love Christ enough to die to the centrality of his role in the church. He must become the coach, the teacher and pastor of the laymen who will be the new focus of attention in the developing renewal movement.[6]

If this basic idea is accepted, that the laity are called to *diakonia* and especially *marturia*, and that the distinctive *diakonia* of the clergy is to train them for it, let me illustrate this principle from our experience in London, first regarding the training of the laity and secondly regarding their service.

THE TRAINING OF THE LAITY

Before I come to the details of the lay training scheme which we have tried to develop, I think I need to enforce a little more the necessity of a training programme of some kind. I have myself found it helpful to remember that our Lord's own ministry was a balanced one. He divided His time between preaching to multitudes, counselling individuals and training the twelve. Most clergy are involved in the first two – preaching to the congregation and interviewing individual people; it is

[1] Trueblood: *The Incendiary Fellowship*, p. 36
[2] *especially* Robert Raines: *New Life in the Church* (Harper and Row, 1963) and Thomas Mullen: *The Renewal of the Ministry* (Abingdon, 1963)
[3] Trueblood: *The Incendiary Fellowship*, p. 41
[4] Trueblood: *The Incendiary Fellowship*, p. 42
[5] Trueblood: *The Incendiary Fellowship*, p. 143
[6] Keith Miller: *The Taste of New Wine*, p. 111-113

the third which we tend to neglect. It is quite true that the training of the apostles was a unique ministry. Yet the principle of giving to a select group of potential leaders a more intensive course of instruction seems still to apply today. I think we may say that a ministry of preaching and counselling, to the exclusion of group training, is an unbalanced ministry, for it does not follow the pattern of Christ's.

Certainly the responsibility of the clergy to train the laity has been increasingly recognized in the Anglican Communion. Archbishop Temple is quoted in *Towards the Conversion of England* as saying that 'the main duty of the clergy must be to train the lay members of the congregation in their work of witness'.[1] Similarly, Archbishop Cyril Garbett wrote in *The Claims of the Church of England*: 'no effort should be spared to build up in every parish a band of lay men and women who are not only devoted to their church but who can give an intelligent reason for their membership'.[2] In 1954 at Evanston, the Second Assembly of the World Council of Churches made this statement:

> the laity stand at the very outposts of the Kingdom of God. They are the missionaries of Christ in every secular sphere. Theirs is the task to carry the message of the Church into every area of life, to be informed and courageous witnesses to the will of our Lord in the world. To this end they will need training and guidance.[3]

And now Lambeth 1968 has added its own earnest appeal:

> No-one wants untrained troops. Anglicans pay lip service to training, but in fact it has generally stopped by the age of fifteen. We need a Christian education explosion comparable to that in the secular world (p. 97).

Hence Resolution 27:

> The Conference believes that there is an urgent need for increase in the quantity and quality of training available for laypeople for their task in the world (p. 38).

But are the laity ready and willing to be trained? Are they not already overpressed by multitudinous activities? Can we really expect them to undertake a course of serious training, followed by responsible service? I believe the answer to these questions is that if the laity to whom we are referring are truly Christian, that is, personally committed to Jesus Christ as their Saviour and Lord, then they are not only ready but eager to serve Him, and that they are disappointed, frustrated and even spiritually wounded, if we do not help them to fulfil their God-given calling to be active witnesses to Jesus Christ.

We have now held a Training School at All Souls every year since 1950. During this time the average annual number of successful candidates has been nearly 43. This does not mean (I hasten to add) that the 718 who have so far been commissioned are all still active. The position at the present time is that only 166 are. The rest have had to resign their commission, mostly through leaving London. Many of these are now serving in other churches, while a number are in the ordained ministry or on the mission field. But it is interesting that the average number of years of service given by those still active is about five-and-a-half, and I learn from the questionnaire recently submitted to them (which 103 of them completed) that on average they spend nearly three hours a week on the particular church work which has been assigned to them. All this seems to be clear evidence of the keenness of lay people to be equipped for active service in the Church. 'I received great blessing from the Lord when attending the Confirmation Classes', wrote one of them, a Health Visitor, 'and then had a great inward desire to serve Him in some way'. So she enrolled in the Training School and is now engaged in house-to-house visitation.

How, then, are the laity to be trained? In one sense, if the ministry of the Church is faithful, they are being trained all the time. That is to say, one cannot distinguish rigidly between 'teaching' and 'training', and every pastor's ambition, through the regular ministry of Word and sacrament, through coun-

---

[1] *Towards the Conversion of England*, p. 36
[2] Garbett: *The Claims of the Church of England*, p. 177
[3] *The Evanston Report*, p. 103

selling and example, is to 'present every man mature in Christ'.[1] Nevertheless, for the work of witness in the parish, especially for such tasks as visiting in people's homes and leading Sunday School or Bible study classes, some extra and more specific training is clearly needed.

Our own training programme, which has to be undertaken before lay people are eligible to engage in parochial *marturia*, is in three stages, first the Annual Training School itself, secondly the examination and thirdly the Commissioning Service.

First, the Training School. This consists of a course of twelve lectures on the theory and practice of evangelism, one evening lecture a week from October to February, with a break over Christmas. An explanatory leaflet is printed, which contains an enrolment form. An open invitation is given to members of the congregation to enrol in the school, while at the same time a more personal approach is made to the previous year's confirmation class and to certain individuals whose spiritual gifts and potentiality have been noticed. The lecture course is divided into two equal halves. The first is entitled 'the theology of the gospel' and introduces the doctrines of God and man, of Jesus Christ, the cross, the Holy Spirit and the Church. The second section is called 'the practice of evangelism' and comprises talks on 'how to be fit for the Master's use', 'how to persevere when discouraged', 'how to lead a friend to Christ', 'how to meet common objections', 'how to speak for Christ' and 'how to visit in homes'. Duplicated lecture summaries are supplied, and loose-leaf notebooks to contain these are on sale. Most of those attending also make notes of their own. We think the school is probably a bit too academic and theoretical, and that more opportunity should be given both to discussion on the one hand and to practical training on the other (although the latter comes later). However, over 86 per cent of those who answered the questionnaire considered the course about right. 'How thrilling and satisfying even limited study of the Word of

56

God can be' was the reaction of an elderly lady candidate, while the comment of a middle-aged bank cashier was: 'pretty tough going, but don't reduce it'.

The next step is the written exam. This is taken by candidates in their own home. We do not attempt to invigilate them, but make it clear that, although they may use their Bible as much as they like, we trust them not to use their lecture summaries or notes or any other aid. Most people have found the exam quite easy. The first question we ask is basic, such as 'what is the gospel?' or 'what is a Christian?', to ensure so far as possible that the candidate himself is a sincere believer. Other sample questions in recent years have been: 'write out in full, with the references, any two verses of Scripture which you might use in explaining to an enquirer the steps to Christ'. 'Summarize *either* the evidence for the deity of Jesus *or* the work of the Holy Spirit.' 'What are the chief motives for evangelism?' 'Give a brief reply to the following remarks: "Science has disproved the Bible." "The Church is full of hypocrites." "I'm perfectly happy as I am." "I can't reconcile all the suffering of the world with a God of love." "I'm just not interested." '

The written exam is followed by a personal interview which provides an opportunity both for going through the corrected exam paper and for a personal assessment of the candidate. At the same time some discussion takes place about the particular kind of service which each will undertake. This is decided by mutual agreement, in the light of the current needs and the candidate's ability, experience and preference.

It might be thought that the setting of this combined written and oral examination would constitute an ordeal sufficiently distasteful to put many people off. But we have not found this to be so. Probably we should be more flexible in allowing some people (who are, for example, more elderly or more experienced or less educated) to qualify without the necessity of a written exam. And indeed we already make some exceptions, but the

[1] Colossians 1.28

general rule has stood the test of time, and over 95 per cent agreed in the questionnaire with the rightness of having one. They see its value in providing an incentive to study and revision, in helping to consolidate knowledge and crystallize thought, and in judging the fitness of each candidate for service in the parish.

Next comes the commissioning service, which takes place on a midweek evening, sometimes in church, sometimes more informally in a hall. Our bishop has been kind enough to come each year for it. After a few questions modelled on the ordination services, touching the candidates' fitness, sense of call and undertaking to be faithful, the Bishop uses the following words of commissioning: 'may the love of God the Father encompass you. May the presence of God the Son uphold you. May the power of God the Holy Spirit rest upon you. Go forth in the name of God, as the ambassadors of Christ and the servants of men, and may the Lord bless your labours abundantly.' Prayers and a blessing conclude the service, after which each receives his commissioning certificate. Some people find the service too formal and impersonal, but most agree that it increases the candidates' sense of the importance and privilege of the service they will do. It has often been a truly solemn occasion. 'I really felt I had been commissioned', wrote one person afterwards. It is interesting to read the concern expressed in the Lambeth 1968 Report 'at the lack of any form of commissioning for laymen analogous to the ordination of clergy' (p. 99). Resolution 25 recommends an exploration of the theology of baptism and confirmation 'in relation to the need to commission the laity for their task in the world' (p. 37).

We do not of course imagine that a fairly elementary course of twelve lectures, even if it is followed by an examination and a commissioning, is an adequate training for all forms of Christian service. But it is at least a basic minimum. It is also supplemented by three or four meetings for all Commissioned Workers each year, in which some further instruction is given and through which a continuing cohesion is given to the work. But more specialized training is attempted for groups like Sunday School teachers, and it seems clear that further advance along this line is needed.

The index of Commissioned Workers is constantly kept up to date. It is generally understood both that certain tasks in the work of the Church are 'commissioned service', which may only be performed by those who have been commissioned, and that if a commissioned worker gives up his commissioned service (unless he transfers to another branch of it) he must resign his commission.

THE SERVICE OF THE LAITY

We turn now from the training of the laity to the service of the laity. What tasks do commissioned workers undertake? They are many and varied. But since they are all forms of *marturia* and involve relationship to *people*, perhaps the best classification is in terms of the people to whom the witness is borne.

The first and largest group is the residents of the parish – nearly 9,000 of them according to the latest census. Since it is the general duty of every church to take the gospel to the people who do not come to hear it, and since it is the particular duty of every Church of England church to care for the souls of the parish, we have always tried to emphasize the importance of house-to-house visitation. Most commissioned workers begin their service by doing at least a year of this kind of visiting. The parish has been divided into three geographical areas, each with a District Superintendent and a group of visitors. These go out two by two, like the Twelve and the Seventy, into the homes of the street or block allocated to them. It should be clearly understood that their objective in visiting is not to canvass for money, nor just to make a friendly social call from the church, nor even (at least in the first instance) to invite the people to come to church, but to be witnesses to Jesus Christ.

This does not mean that they will be rude or brash or tactless. It may well take them time to win people's confidence before it would be right or wise for them to witness. They may also leave Christian literature and invite those visited to a special Guest Service or meeting. But they do not forget their primary responsibility, which is themselves to speak of Jesus Christ.

At the time of writing, we have just been giving further thought to the objective of this house-to-house visiting. Have we been right to define it almost exclusively in terms of witness? The National Evangelical Anglican Congress Statement affirmed that 'Evangelism and compassionate service belong together in the mission of God'.[1] What, then, should be the response of house-to-house visitors to some social need which they discover, such as a marriage breakdown, or unemployment, or a financial crisis or a defaulting landlord? Should they become involved in such things? Or would this social involvement distract them from their evangelistic task? After full discussion we have been brought to a common mind about this question. House-to-house visitors have always tried to lend a helping hand in situations of social need, but now we have clarified their responsibility. We are bringing into being a new group of Commissioned Workers to be called 'Welfare Visitors', to whom a case of social need may be referred, but only in certain circumstances. House-to-house visitors are not merely witnesses. They are also Christians! So because Christians are called to love and by love to serve,[2] and because the visitors enter homes as Christian people, they must keep their eyes open for social as well as spiritual need, and they must have liberty to seek to meet whatever need they find. Only if some situation is likely to demand more time or more specialist knowledge than they have at their disposal, are they encouraged to call in a Welfare Visitor.

Door-to-door visiting is arduous and exacting. Tramping the streets and climbing the steep stairs of tenement blocks is tiring after a hard day's work in the office. Many homes are occupied by foreign visitors or immigrants – Cypriot, Chinese, Italian, Pakistani – and the language barrier proves a formidable obstacle. Often the TV is on, and the visitors are made to feel unwelcome. In some cases the reception is worse than cool; it is actively hostile. But perhaps the clearest impression gained by the visitors is the size of the gulf in contemporary England which separates the masses from the Church. 'People are self-satisfied and do not want to know of Christ', writes one. There is 'deep misunderstanding' of Christian truth, says another, while people's objections are more often based on hearsay than on personal conviction. A third speaks of 'the widespread and appalling ignorance of the gospel', which she has discovered in her visiting.

So this visiting is tough. Many visitors have declared that the biggest lessons which they themselves have learned through their commissioned service are the need for 'patience and endurance', for 'tolerance', for 'boldness' or 'self-discipline' or 'compassion', while others have come to see with limpid clarity that 'the conversion of souls is the Holy Spirit's work', and that 'unless we go in God's strength we are powerless'. Although we have tried to encourage the visitors by periodical Visiting Campaigns, in which members of the church staff join, and by a Parish Survey, in which the use of a questionnaire has opened up many conversations, we still recognize what a difficult labour this visiting is, requiring strong Christian qualities of perseverance and a constant, humble reliance on the Holy Spirit Himself.

Yet there have also been a number of encouragements. Several visitors have spoken of 'the joy of being able to speak to people about Christ' or 'the joy of being able to witness, sometimes spending over an hour with people, being bombarded with questions, and having real peace even when not knowing all the answers!' Others have been surprised by the spiritual

[1] *Keele '67*, p. 23, paragraph 20
[2] Galatians 5.13

receptivity of some people they have visited. When 'talking to people about the Lord Jesus Christ', one described 'how willing most of them are to listen to us'. And some could testify to the thrill of 'seeing someone we visited eventually coming to love the Lord'.

A second group of people, for whom the Church has a special responsibility, is the elderly and the sick. We have a small group of sick visitors who attend a monthly Service of Prayer for the Sick and are asked, in particular, to pray for and visit some who are chronically ill. There is a much larger group of 'Old People's Welfare Visitors'. Instead of going in pairs from door to door like the house-to-house visitors, these Old People's Welfare Visitors go singly and regularly to visit just one or two old-age pensioners. As a group they too have a Superintendent, who is in touch with the local Old People's Welfare Association and the various services for old people provided by the Borough. Being called 'Old People's *Welfare* Visitors', their concern is for the total welfare of those they visit, spiritual as well as physical and social. The practical tasks they are able to perform are innumerable, ranging from letter-writing, shopping, cooking and pension problems, to the provision of wireless for the bedridden, spectacles, dentures and fracture boards.

This visiting is exacting also. Each visitor has to learn to be a good listener. One speaks of 'the joy and the heartache of sharing the ups and downs in the life of the old lady' she visits. One or two are visiting hardened atheists and find it a great trial to persevere in love and friendship towards them. But others can tell of real blessing. 'Some of the folk I have visited have become very dear friends', says one. Another writes of 'the joy of loving, giving to, sharing with and serving the old ladies' whom she visits. Another has learned from this visiting that 'it is in giving that we truly receive'. What do they receive? This is what they say is their reward: 'the increasing faith and holiness in some old people', or 'seeing Miss W.'s face when she opens the door', while another declares 'I feel Mrs C. has a greater desire for spiritual things than I; she exhorts me now!' It is often touching to observe the loving care extended to these old folk, as a result of which seven or more of them are being looked after in a small Old People's Home which our church opened in the parish seven years ago.

The third group among whom commissioned workers are labouring is children and young people. Some are Sunday School teachers, others help with a Sunday morning Family Service, and others are club leaders in the parochial Community Centre which has been operating since 1958. In it a full range of clubs is provided for all ages, with emphasis on young people. Those who work in the Clubhouse (as it is called) are divided into 'club leaders' and 'club helpers'. Club helpers do trojan service in the canteen and the office and in other practical ways, but do not need to be commissioned. Club leaders are all commissioned, however, and exercise a spiritual responsibility in the clubs they lead. They work together as a team, and although they have some disciplinary and other problems, they can also bear witness to a living God who is at work in their midst. One club leader says 'I have found that giving out love has enriched my own life'. A Sunday School teacher finds it specially rewarding to see 'small children really understand important truths, for instance when they start to pray themselves instead of just repeating what they have heard from adults', while another club leader has been deeply impressed 'to see the teenagers change when they have accepted Christ'.

Fourthly, some commissioned workers are seeking to serve the young Christians of the congregation, the babes of God's family, the lambs of Christ's flock. Those who come forward in response to the invitation given at the monthly Guest Service are all counselled, and every counsellor is, of course, a commissioned worker. We then invite them into a so-called 'Nursery Class'. We find the title a trifle embarrassing, but none the less we have never succeeded in changing it. At least it has the merit of accuracy, since the Nursery Class is designed for newborn babes in Christ, who are still at the nursery stage. Each Nursery Class meets weekly. It is intended to help spiritual babes to take their first simple steps in Bible reading and prayer, and to begin to draw them into the Church's fellowship. There are now seven Nursery Classes, meeting on different days of the week and at different times, and most of the leaders and assistant leaders are lay people and again commissioned workers. Perhaps they have the greatest privilege of all in commissioned service, because they are allowed to watch God evidently at work in human lives. One Nursery Class leader describes the wonderful joy of seeing 'the miracle of the new birth and growth of the young Christian', while the leader of a Secondary Class (to which many Nursery Class members graduate) mentions the similar joy of 'seeing spiritual babes grow to manhood'.

Not that every new Christian joins a Nursery Class or that everyone who does stays the course. There are disappointments and discouragements in this branch of service too. One Nursery Class leader has specially learned, she says, that 'all efforts to cajole or persuade people to attend are worse than useless if you don't *pray*'.

The fifth group whom commissioned workers try to serve I will call 'strangers' – strangers to London and especially strangers from overseas. Being a London church, we receive a steady stream of letters from all over the world, from grannies and aunties, parents and cousins, clergy and friends, telling us that someone is arriving in London and asking us if we will make contact with them. To such we want to show that *philoxenia* ('love for strangers' or 'hospitality') which is required of Christian people.[1] So we have a small group of commissioned workers, called 'sponsors' for want of a better name, whose task is to get in touch with a person commended to us, befriend him, invite him to church and/or a midweek activity, introduce him to others, and stand by him until he feels that he really belongs to the fellowship.

The largest number of such 'strangers' comes from overseas.

These include visitors on vacation, business people, *au pair* girls and especially students. Most of the latter come to do work in the University (17 per cent of whose student body is from overseas) and in other colleges, a significant number of them undertaking some kind of advanced graduate study. In order to help us to care for them we appointed a layman in 1963 as 'Counsellor to Overseas Visitors'. He is responsible for the church's International Fellowship.

A team of commissioned workers shares the ministry with him, especially in the leadership of a number of international Bible study groups. On the whole, they find it exciting work. 'If we try to do it in our own strength', write a young married couple who are leaders of one such group, 'we get flustered and frustrated. We have learned to trust the Lord to help us.' When they do use spiritual weapons in spiritual work, they add, they have the joy of 'seeing "shaky" Christians mature and their faith deepen'.

The sixth group of people among whom commissioned workers labour are ordinary members of the congregation. Large numbers of them belong to small Fellowship Groups, nearly all of which have lay leaders, all of whom, together with their deputy leaders, are Commissioned Workers. I will not delay on their responsibilities now, because the next chapter will be devoted to this subject.

This, then, is an approximate classification of commissioned service. Commissioned workers are engaged in the systematic visitation of parishioners, the chronic sick and the elderly; in the teaching and training of the young; in the nurture of new Christians; in the care of strangers, and in the pastoral oversight of church members.

AN EVALUATION

Looking back over the seventeen years in which this programme

[1] *for instance*, Romans 12.13

of the training, examining, commissioning and service of the laity has been operating, we are perhaps in a position to make a critical assessment of it. What are its weaknesses, and what are its values?

I think the first weakness has been in the realm of inadequate supervision. Twenty-five of those who answered the questionnaire mentioned this in one way or another. The Sunday School, Clubhouse and International Fellowship workers seem to belong to closely knit and well supervised groups, but some of the visitors, especially the house-to-house visitors who are in the front-line of the church's advance into the parish, feel they need more support, not least from the clergy. I do not believe this is a lingering clericalism which is to be resisted, but rather a genuine desire that lay commissioned service will be in partnership with the work of the clergy and not a substitute for it. I myself have only recently learned that the true art of delegation is not to hand over work to somebody else and then forget about it, but to commit work to a deputy who knows that he is responsible to you and can at times report back and seek advice.

The second weakness, like the first, is a danger to which the scheme is prone, rather than an inevitable and intrinsic weakness. It is, in fact, a danger to which the administration of every kind of spiritual work is exposed. It concerns the relation between form and spirit, between organization and freedom. It is possible that the training-examining-commissioning sequence actually inhibits the free enterprise of those not commissioned, because they may feel they have no liberty to work for Christ if they are not commissioned. In this situation we need to insist strongly that Christian people are perfectly free to fulfil their duties to witness and engage in other forms of Christian activity without waiting to be organized into it by the local church or needing official permission to begin it! The purposes of training and commissioning are to encourage, improve and co-ordinate the service of the laity in the local church and parish, not to frustrate it or quench the Spirit.

Turning from the weaknesses and perils of this scheme to its advantages, I think we may say that it has a threefold value.

First, it makes possible genuine teamwork between clergy and laity in *diakonia*. It encourages the laity to bear the witness to which God calls them – 'the joy of serving the Lord and making Him known to others', as one describes it, and it enables the clergy to fulfil their God-given role in helping to equip them for it.

Secondly, if the scheme encourages some, it also discourages others. And this is necessary. As one of our more senior commissioned workers has expressed it, herself holding an Inter-Diocesan Certificate: 'it has encouraged many diffident Christians to undertake active service for which they would never have offered themselves . . . and perhaps checked some who would have been too self assertive'. This negative value of the scheme is more important than may at first sight appear. Would it be an exaggeration to say that one of the scandals of the contemporary ecclesiastical scene is the number of unsuitable and uninstructed people who are teaching in the Church's Sunday Schools? I do not think this an overstatement. Many teachers are, of course, well qualified and deeply devoted; but many others are quite unsure of themselves, their faith and their personal relationship to Jesus Christ. Now one good thing which the training and commissioning arrangement has done for us is firmly and finally to close the back door into the privileged service of the Church. If anybody now volunteers to visit or teach or counsel, one can say 'Fine! The Training School begins in October.' Surely a responsible church *must* ensure that its accredited visitors, teachers, leaders and counsellors have received at least a modicum of training? They represent Christ and His Church; they need to be equipped for this honourable service. I was relieved and heartened to find in the questionnaire that, in answer to the question 'do you approve or disapprove of our insistence on training and commissioning before anybody is entrusted with spiritual church work?' 96 per cent of those who replied said they approved, the great majority emphatically and wholeheartedly.

The third value of the scheme which is worth a mention concerns the 'status' which a commissioned worker enjoys. True, all 'status' has its perils, and fallen human beings even if born again and baptized into Christ are not exempt from temptations to pride and jealousy. True also, it is quite possible for training to be given and service to be rendered without any episcopal commissioning. Nevertheless, a number of commissioned workers have realized the advantages of commissioning. Some acknowledge that their position has helped them to take their work more seriously, to be disciplined in it and to realize their commitment to the service to which they have been assigned. Others have found in their commissioning not so much an incentive for themselves as a certain authority in the eyes of others, especially as a means of entry into people's homes. 'It gives me confidence', one has written 'to know that I go as a representative, and with the support, of the Church.'

Let me conclude this chapter with a clarification: the particular pattern of Training School and commissioned service which we have developed is certainly no stereotype for every other church – especially those in different situations. It is entirely dispensable. But the training and the service of the laity are not. These are indispensable, at least in any church which seeks to conform its life to New Testament teaching. What matters is the fundamental principle of the laity's *marturia*, and their need of the clergy's *diakonia* in equipping them for it; the precise pattern in which this principle is expressed may vary in every church.

4

The Christian Fellowship *(koinonia)*

WE began by insisting that a proper understanding of the laity depends on a proper understanding of the Church, and that the primary purpose of the biblical church-metaphors is to illustrate not the relations of clergy and laity within the Church but the relations of all God's people to Himself and to each other. The latter, our mutual relations as Christian people, are usually referred to in terms of 'fellowship', and it is on the meaning and implications of the Christian fellowship that we shall concentrate in this final chapter.

'Fellowship' is an overworked word in the contemporary Church, and the image conveyed by it is often a false image. Indeed, the vocabulary of fellowship has become such devalued currency that it seldom means more than a genial mateyness, what Methodists call a 'P.S.A.' (Pleasant Sunday Afternoon) or a good gossipy get-together over a nice cup of tea. As a result, we fall sadly short of the rich, deep, full fellowship envisaged in the New Testament.

Yet strong forces are at work towards its recovery – biblical, historical and practical.

ARGUMENTS FOR FELLOWSHIP

To begin with, we have good biblical warrant for asserting that it is not good for man to be alone[1] – an affirmation which at least Calvin saw had a wider reference than to marriage. Aloneness is not the will of God either in ordinary life or in the Christian life. People need fellowship (which we shall still for

[1] *see* Genesis 2.18

the moment leave undefined), and it is God's will that they should have it. 'The real menace to life in the world today', wrote M. E. Macdonald 'is not the hydrogen bomb . . . but the fact of proximity without community.'[1]

Bruce Larson, the leader of the American 'Faith at Work' movement, sees an indication of this fundamental human need in the popularity of the pub:

> The neighbourhood bar is possibly the best counterfeit there is to the fellowship Christ wants to give His Church. It's an imitation, dispensing liquor instead of grace, escape rather than reality, but it is a permissive, accepting and inclusive fellowship. It is unshockable. It is democratic. You can tell people secrets and they usually don't tell others or even want to. The bar flourishes not because most people are alcoholics, but because God has put into the human heart the desire to know and be known, to love and be loved, and so many seek a counterfeit at the price of a few beers. Christ wants His Church to be unshockable, democratic, permissive – a fellowship where people can come in and say 'I'm sunk!' 'I'm beat!' 'I've had it!' Alcoholics Anonymous has this quality. Our churches too often miss it.[2]

But this basic, biblically recognized need is not completely met by Sunday churchgoing or even the larger midweek meetings of the church. There is always something unnatural and subhuman about large crowds. They tend to be aggregations rather than congregations – aggregations of unrelated persons. The larger they become, the less the individuals who compose them know and care about each other. Indeed, crowds can actually perpetuate aloneness, instead of curing it. There is a need, therefore, for large congregations to be divided into smaller groups, such as one imagines the house-churches were in New Testament days.[3] The value of the small group is that it can become a community of related persons; and in it the benefit of personal relatedness cannot be missed, nor its challenge evaded.

This is true of the human family. Our growth into maturity, according to the purpose of God, takes place in the context of a family group. It is the complex pattern of relationships between parents, children, brothers and sisters which, more than anything else, governs our development into adult stature. It is the only child who often suffers, although even in his case there is a unit of three, not to mention relatives, neighbours and friends. Similarly, it is the lone member of the congregation, who holds himself aloof from a more intimate Christian fellowship, who is likely to stunt or damage his spiritual progress.

I do not think it is an exaggeration to say, therefore, that small groups, Christian family or fellowship groups, are indispensable for our growth into spiritual maturity. The preservation of lone-wolf Christianity is perfectly possible for the churchgoer who sits isolated in a pew or hides behind a pillar, even if he attends a so-called midweek 'fellowship' where large numbers again gather. His baptism has made him a member of the visible community. By his church attendance he becomes an outwardly conforming member. But still he may not truly belong either to Christ or to the people of Christ.

Turning from a biblical to a historical argument for small groups, we may say that many famous movements of the Spirit of God have either begun or expressed themselves in the intimacy of such fellowship. This is certainly true of the English Reformation, whose roots can be traced to the group of scholars who met in the White Horse Inn in Cambridge to study Erasmus' Greek Testament. It is also true of Methodism, whether one thinks of the original Holy Club in Oxford or of the class meetings of the developed Society. Reference could also be made to the Praying Societies of Scotland and to the fellowship meetings of the current East African revival. It is from such small and unpretentious beginnings that great movements have sprung up and spread.

The third argument is pastoral. In every congregation of any size there is a need for better and more personal pastoral over-

[1] M. E. Macdonald: *The Need To Believe* (Fontana, 1959), p. 82
[2] Larson: *Dare To Live Now!*, p. 110
[3] *for instance*, Romans 16.3–5; Philemon 1–2

sight. The clergy tend to concentrate on nurturing the new convert, visiting the sick, interviewing those to be baptized, confirmed or married, comforting the bereaved, counselling those who ask for help and training workers for witness. But they cannot hope to see or visit every member of their congregation regularly, at least if it is at all sizeable. Nor indeed should they. The pastoral oversight of the congregation does not belong exclusively to the ordained ministry. The Church of Scotland is quite right to have lay elders who share this responsibility with the minister, and one admires the enterprise of the Rev. Roy Henderson who introduced a lay eldership scheme when he was Vicar of St Luke's, Barton Hill, Bristol. He wrote in the *Church of England Newspaper* on 9 June 1967: 'We have lay elders who have been duly appointed by the Bishop to share in the leadership and pastoral care of the parish.' With one exception they are local men already well known to and respected by the congregation.

Moreover, the Bible indicates that each of us is his brother's keeper. It even hints that in one sense every Christian may be regarded as a bishop, because a certain *episcope* ('oversight') is entrusted to every member of the congregation. 'See to it', we are told in Hebrews 12.15, where the verb is *episkopountes*, 'that no one fail to obtain the grace of God.' If this is so, it is in fellowship groups that the ideal can become a reality, for in these the minister delegates some *episcope* or pastoral oversight to the lay leaders, and all learn to care for each.

This is what John Wesley found. On 25 April 1742 he recorded in his Journal:

> I appointed several earnest and sensible men to meet me, to whom I showed the great difficulty I had long found of knowing the people who desired to be under my care. After much discourse, they all agreed there could be no better way to come to a sure, thorough knowledge of each person than to divide them into classes, like those at Bristol, under the inspection of those in whom I could most confide. This was the origin of our classes at London, for which I can never sufficiently praise God, the

unspeakable usefulness of the institution having ever since been more and more manifest.[1]

And Dr R. W. Dale commented on this procedure:

Methodism made one striking and original contribution to the institutions of the Church, in the Class-meeting. Never, so far as I know, in any church had there been so near an approach to the ideal of pastoral oversight as the Class-meeting, in its perfect form, provides; and it also provides for that communion of saints which is almost as necessary for the strength and joy and the harmonious growth of the Christian life as fellowship with God.[2]

Certainly in our own generation, at least since the end of the Second World War, the house-church or home-group movement has been steadily gathering momentum in many parts of the world. In most cases it has no articulated biblical, historical or pastoral rationale. It seems to be largely spontaneous, a genuine movement of the Holy Spirit. If it needs to be explained in terms of human experience, it is probably to be understood as a protest against the dehumanizing processes of secular society and the superficial formalism of much church life. There is a widespread hunger for a life which is genuinely human and absolutely real.

One such spontaneous movement is taking place among business and professional people in south-west Texas. Keith Miller writes about it in *The Taste of New Wine*. His book's title expresses the heady experience of Christian commitment. These laymen are 'no longer satisfied merely to sit in the pews and on committees or even to stand in pulpits' (p. 18). Their new life in Christ is like new and fermenting wine, which threatens to burst the old wineskins of the institutional church (p. 105–116). In particular, these men are seeking to live their lives whole and not to departmentalize their Christianity. 'Christ is tearing out the partitions in men's souls between vocation, church and home, and making a one-room dwelling place for Himself in

[1] quoted in Leslie F. Church: *The Early Methodist People* (Epworth, 1948), p. 155
[2] Church: *The Early Methodist People*, p. 153

their whole lives' (p. 18). Keith Miller describes the shock it was when, after he had been a church member and church worker for many years, a business colleague said to him 'Gee, Keith, I didn't know you were a Christian':

> This stunned me into realizing that, although I had taken Christ by the hand and led Him through one passage after another in the labyrinth of my soul, I had always left Him at the parking lot when I drove in to go to my office in the major oil company for which I worked (p. 79).

It came to him that the lordship of Christ must be allowed to penetrate every part of his life:

> I didn't have to have a separate vocabulary, a different kind of humour and a different set of ethics for my business life, my church life, my family life and my prayer life (p. 65).

So he invited eleven or twelve people 'who seemed most hungry to know God' to join him in a group. Together they determined to make the experiment 'to take Christ consciously through the routine of our days and nights' and to report back to one another. Each time they met, they engaged in Bible study and prayer, but in addition they shared 'the problems and discoveries' of the past week, and so began to trace 'the fresh and contemporary footprints of Christ' in their own lives (p. 70, 71). Individually they became involved in sick visiting, in questions of integration and business life, in the fostering of a Cuban refugee boy and in the after-care of prisoners. But the greatest discovery they made is that Christianity is

> not a 'religion' at all, but *real* creative life, life in which we are free to be honest about ourselves, and to accept and love each other and Him, because the Living Christ is in the midst of us . . . winning us to Himself and to His world (p. 75).

I had the great pleasure of meeting Keith Miller in Texas in January 1968 and of hearing him amplify what I had read in his book. What intrigued us both is that we in London had brought into being similar groups with similar aims, although we had begun from the other end. That is to say, Keith Miller and his friends had formed their groups out of a felt need, whereas we (though also aware of the need) had done so from theological conviction, from a study of what the New Testament means by *koinonia*, fellowship.

THE BIBLICAL MEANING OF *koinonia*

At the heart of *koinonia* is the basic word *koinos*, common. And the nouns *koinonia* (fellowship) and *koinonos* (a partner), together with the verb *koinoneo* (to share) all bear witness to what we have in common. Thus C. H. Dodd writes: '*koinonoi* are persons who hold property in common, partners or shareholders in a common concern'.[1]

A careful study of the New Testament use of this word-group indicates that Christian *koinonia* or 'commonness' takes three forms.

First and foremost, there is what we share in together, our common Christian inheritance. Indeed this is the fundamental meaning of the word. In usual parlance today 'fellowship' describes something subjective, an awareness or an experience of belonging together. 'We had good fellowship together', we say, indicating our sense of warmth and security in each other's company. But in the Bible 'fellowship' is an objective fact. *Koinonia* bears witness to our common possession of the blessings of the gospel. We have a 'common faith' and therefore a 'common salvation', being 'joint partakers (*sugkoinonous*) of grace'.[2] Faith, salvation and grace are the common denominator among Christians; each of us has been saved by grace through faith.[3] It is this that makes us one.

In particular, we share in the saving grace of the three

[1] C. H. Dodd: *Moffatt Commentary on the Johannine Epistles* (Hodder and Stoughton, 1946), p. 6
[2] Titus 1.4; Jude 3; Philippians 1.7
[3] Ephesians 2.8–9

persons of the Trinity. Thus, through the witness of the apostles we come to have fellowship with them, and their fellowship is 'with the Father and with His Son Jesus Christ'.[1] Indeed, our 'fellowship with one another' is dependent on our 'fellowship with Him'.[2] Next, we have been 'called' by God 'into the fellowship of his Son, Jesus Christ our Lord', and through the breaking of the loaf and the blessing of the cup we enjoy a communion or participation (*koinonia*) in His body and blood.[3] Further, we are granted 'the fellowship of the Holy Spirit', who dwells in all the people of God and makes them 'partakers (*koinonoi*) of the divine nature'.[4]

Begotten by the will and word of the same Father, redeemed by the blood of the same Son, indwelt by the presence of the same Spirit – this is our *koinonia*, the 'common salvation' in which we have all come by grace through faith to share.

Not that we can now relax in sloth or sin. For such fellowship with God who is light is itself an incentive to holiness, precluding fellowship with or participation in 'the unfruitful works of darkness'.[5] Moreover, salvation does not exempt us from suffering. On the contrary, fellowship with Christ includes 'the fellowship of His sufferings'. But those who 'share Christ's sufferings' will also share in 'the glory that is to be revealed', so that all Christians are companions in, or partakers (in Jesus) of, both 'the tribulation and the kingdom and the patient endurance'.[6]

Such is the fundamental meaning of *koinonia*, a common participation in grace now and in glory hereafter, though also of suffering meanwhile. Christian fellowship is our common share in God's 'great salvation'.[7]

But fellowship is more than what we share *in* together. There is also and secondly, what we share *out* together. For *koinonia* in the New Testament concerns not only what we possess but what we do together, not only our common inheritance but also our common service. Luke uses the word *koinonoi* to describe the business relationship between the two pairs of brothers James and John, Andrew and Simon. They were 'partners', he says.[8] C. H. Dodd explains this as meaning that they were 'joint owners of the little fishing fleet', but it surely means also that they were colleagues, engaged together in the same fishing trade.

After the apostles had successfully landed their great netful of fish, Jesus said to Simon 'Do not be afraid; henceforth you will be catching men'. It is perhaps, therefore, not too fanciful to regard the church as a great fellowship of fishermen, *koinonoi*, partners with Jesus Christ and with one another in the business of catching men. Certainly Paul refers to his co-labourers Titus and Philemon as his *koinonoi*, and specially mentions how Philemon shared out his faith with others.[9] But it was not only such Christian leaders who were Paul's companions in labour. He could thank God for the Philippian Christians' 'partnership in the gospel', which had persisted 'from the first day' (of their conversion) until the time of his writing to them.[10] The preposition *eis* (rendered here 'in') makes it plain that their partnership was in the spread of the gospel, not just in the enjoyment of its benefits. A similar use of the word *koinonia* in relation to the preaching of the gospel occurs in Galatians 2.9. Here Paul describes how the Jerusalem apostles, James, Peter and John, gave to him and to Barnabas 'the right hand of fellowship'. What did this gesture indicate? It was a token of partnership in world evangelization, signifying 'that we should go to the Gentiles and they to the circumcised'.

The gospel is not the only treasure, however, which Christians

[1] 1 John 1.1–4; *compare* Acts 2.42
[2] 1 John 1.7, 6
[3] 1 Corinthians 1.9; 10.16; *compare* 10.20
[4] 2 Corinthians 13.14; Philippians 2.1; 2 Peter 1.4
[5] Ephesians 5.11; *compare* 2 Corinthians 6.14; Matthew 23.30; 1 Timothy 5.22; 2 John 11; Revelation 18.4
[6] Philippians 3.10 (AV); 1 Peter 4.13; 5.1; Revelation 1.9; *compare* 2 Corinthians 1.7; Hebrews 10.33
[7] Hebrews 2.3
[8] Luke 5.10
[9] 2 Corinthians 8.23; Philemon 17.6
[10] Philippians 1.5; *compare* 1 Corinthians 9.23

have to share out together. Another is our material possessions. Rich people are to be specially *koinonikos* 'generous',[1] and all Christians are told not to neglect *koinonia*,[2] but rather to 'contribute (*koinoneo*) to the needs of the saints'.[3] And *koinonia* is the word Paul employs for the 'contribution' of the Macedonian and Achaian churches to the poor saints at Jerusalem.[4] Thus *koinonia* seems to express as much our joint-communication of, as our joint-participation in, the blessings of the gospel.

In these first two aspects of *koinonia*, which we have been considering, one might say that Christian people are all facing in one of two directions. When we concentrate on what we share in or possess together, we are all facing the Lord who has given Himself to us. When we concentrate on what we share out or do together, we are all facing other people – either the world or the church – whom we are seeking to serve. But the third aspect of *koinonia* concerns what we share with one another, and when we concentrate on this, we are no longer facing in the same direction: we are gathered in a circle, facing each other. Dr Fitchett once reminded a Canadian audience that

> there are two ideas of the religious life. There is the tramcar idea and the fireside idea. In the tramcar you sit beside your fellow-passenger. You are all going in the same direction, but you have no fellowship, no intercourse with or interest in one another. . . . Then there is the fireside, where the family meet together, where they are at home, where they converse one with another of common pursuits and common interests, and where a common relationship binds all together in a warm bond of love and fellowship. . . . Methodism stands for the fireside idea.[5]

But the 'fireside idea' should not be allowed to be a Methodist monopoly. It is an indispensable characteristic of New Testament *koinonia*. This is not a fellowship in which we are all recipients or all givers, but what Paul calls a 'partnership . . . in giving and receiving'[6] – a verse of Scripture which would have made an admirable text for the Anglican programme of 'MRI'.[7]

This kind of fellowship may be said to have begun on the Day of Pentecost. When Luke wrote of the newly created, believing, Spirit-filled community that they 'had all things in common',[8] he meant that they shared with each other what they had. It was a fellowship of giving and receiving. It would be a mistake, however, to suppose that this third expression of *koinonia* is exclusively concerned with money. For example, the giving and receiving which had taken place between Paul and the Philippians was that he had given them the gospel, while they had sent him a present.[9] Similarly, although the collection among the Greek churches for the poor saints of Judaea was in one sense a free-will offering, it was also the repayment of a debt. Paul saw it as a meaningful symbol of Jewish–Gentile 'MRI', 'for if the Gentiles have come to share in their spiritual blessings, they ought also to be of service to them in material blessings'.[10]

Paul had a strong sense of this mutual responsibility and interdependence between Christians and churches. Although he was himself an apostle of Jesus Christ, bearing Christ's name and gospel before the Gentiles, he was humble enough to acknowledge his need of what others could give him. His Master had once asked an immoral Samaritan woman to give Him a drink of water; and Paul often confessed his need of human friendship.[11] So too in writing to the Romans, although he does not here use the vocabulary of *koinonia*, he says that he longed to visit them not only to impart some spiritual gift to them to strengthen them, but also 'that we may be mutually encouraged by each other's faith, both yours and mine'.[12]

[1] 1 Timothy 6.18
[2] Hebrews 13.16, 'do not neglect . . . to share what you have' (RSV)
[3] Romans 12.13
[4] Romans 15.26; 2 Corinthians 8.4; 9.13
[5] quoted in Church: *The Early Methodist People*, p. 149
[6] Philippians 4.15
[7] 'Mutual Responsibility and Interdependence', a cumbrous expression for the reciprocal aid recommended to the churches by the Anglican Congress at Toronto in 1963
[8] Acts 2.44 (*hapanta koina*); *compare* Acts 4.32
[9] *Compare* Galatians 6.6; 1 Corinthians 9.11
[10] Romans 15.26–27; *compare* Romans 11.7
[11] *for instance*, 2 Corinthians 7.6; 2 Timothy 4.9, 11, 21
[12] Romans 1.11–12

It is in this connection that we need to consider the many 'one another' verses of the New Testament, which describe the reciprocity of true Christian fellowship.

The commonest use of *allelous* 'one another' is of reciprocal love. Jesus said: 'A new commandment I give to you, that you love one another; even as I have loved you, that you also love one another. By this all men will know that you are my disciples, if you have love for one another.' He repeated the command a little later,[1] and we hear echoes of it in the apostolic letters of Paul, Peter and John.[2]

All the remaining 'one another' verses of the New Testament are the outworking – negative and positive – of this mutual love. If we love one another we shall not 'judge' one another, nor 'bite', 'devour', 'provoke' or 'envy' one another, nor 'lie' to one another, nor 'speak evil against' or 'grumble against' one another.[3] True love for one another will express itself positively in a desire to build one another up. This will include 'receiving' one another, being 'kind' and 'tenderhearted' towards one another, forbearing and forgiving one another, 'serving' one another, practising 'hospitality' ungrudgingly to one another, admonishing or instructing one another, submitting to one another, and comforting one another in bereavement.[4]

All this active, purposive service of one another arises from the fundamental fact that we belong to one another. We *are* our brother's keeper precisely because we are brothers. Or, to employ Paul's favourite metaphor, 'we, though many, are one body in Christ, and individually members one of another'.[5] Therefore we must serve one another with the gifts we have received, neither envying nor despising one another, 'that there may be no discord in the body, but that the members may have the same care for one another'. Then, 'if one member suffers, all suffer together; if one member is honoured, all rejoice together'.[6]

Such 'membership one of another' and mutual caring can only be expressed when the members meet in fellowship. So 'greet one another' is another reciprocal duty often repeated in the New Testament epistles,[7] even if the 'holy kiss' with which we do it is today replaced by what J. B. Phillips calls 'a hand-shake all round, please'. If we do not neglect to meet, but actually come together in fellowship, then we are able to 'consider how to stir up one another to love and good works'.[8] Then too we can confess our sins to one another, if we have offended one another, and 'pray for one another'.[9] Again, we can 'bear one another's burdens and so fulfil the law of Christ', for we can 'rejoice with those who rejoice' and 'weep with those who weep'.[10] All this rich and varied 'one anotherness' is an essential part of what the New Testament means by 'fellowship'.

Let me now summarize the threefold aspect which *koinonia* wears in the New Testament. It speaks of our common in-heritance (what we share in together), of our co-operative service (what we share out together) and of our reciprocal responsibility (what we share with one another). In the first we are receiving together, in the second we are giving together, while in the third there is a mutual give and take.

BIBLICAL THEORY AND PAROCHIAL PRACTICE

This is the biblical theory. But an increasing number of Christian people are finding the theory workable. Consider, for example, what has been happening in the Diocese of Coventry since the consecration of its new cathedral. Stephen Verney calls his paperback *Fire in Coventry* 'a book about the Holy

[1] John 13.34–35; 15.12, 17
[2] Romans 12.10; 13.8; 1 Thessalonians 3.12; 4.9; 1 Peter 1.22; 1 John 3.11, 23; 4.7, 11–12; 2 John 5
[3] Romans 14.13; Galatians 5.15, 26; Colossians 3.9; James 4.11; 5.9
[4] Romans 14.19; 15.7; Ephesians 4.2, 32; Colossians 3.13; Galatians 5.13 (*compare* John 13.14); 1 Peter 4.9; Romans 15.14; Ephesians 5.21; 1 Peter 5.5; 1 Thessalonians 4.18
[5] Romans 12.5; *compare* Ephesians 4.25
[6] 1 Corinthians 12.25–26
[7] Romans 16.16; 1 Corinthians 16.20; 2 Corinthians 13.12; 1 Peter 5.14
[8] Hebrews 10.24–25
[9] James 5.16
[10] Galatians 6.2; Romans 12.15

Spirit' (p. 9). It begins with a moving account of how the clergy of Monks Kirby, a suburb of Coventry, became 'a team of men who knew one another, cared about one another, belonged to one another, and most important of all, had begun to admit to one another their own weaknesses' (p. 14). Then their experience of fellowship spread, in successive ripples, reaching both clergy and laity throughout the diocese. Its three elements are analysed as love (which 'goes out to the last and the lost and the least', p. 33), prayer (men putting themselves at God's disposal) and the Holy Spirit. 'These are the three who dance together and are one at the heart of the Church – Love, Prayer, the Holy Spirit. All else is secondary' (p. 51). Stephen Verney depicts them as entering the pages of St John's Gospel 'like three ballet dancers': 'Love one another . . . ask in my name . . . I will give you the Spirit of Truth.' 'First one, then another, holds the centre of the stage; they hold hands and dance together; they weave in and out and through one another in intricate patterns.' He concludes: 'These three dance together and are one, and that one is Jesus Christ. And He gives us all three at once as He gives us Himself . . .' (p. 89–90).

Perhaps I may illustrate the same biblical theory, but in greater detail, from our experience in London. Once our Parochial Church Council had seen and studied the high ideal of Christian fellowship set forth in the New Testament, we were determined to attempt to turn the theory into practice, and to make the ideal a reality. For fifteen years the central meeting of the church each week had been 'the Hour of Prayer'. We had seen it grow from an attendance of about 20 to a maximum of about 200, and then decrease again to a regular 100 or so. But we were dissatisfied with it. It had grown stale. Many who led in prayer were inaudible. Further, it tended to be clerically dominated, and it provided no opportunity for mutual fellowship. In a word, the fellowship it expressed was lop-sided.

So after careful thought and thorough debate the PCC reached the unanimous decision to discontinue it and to transfer the weekly intercession of the Hour of Prayer to fortnightly Fellowship Groups in different homes and (in the alternate weeks) to Parish Evenings, to which the groups would be urged to come together.

In April 1965 a policy statement was issued, which began: 'The staff, churchwardens and PCC have during the last year given a great deal of thought and study to the biblical meaning of Christian fellowship, and to its application to our church life at All Souls. We are convinced from Scripture and history of the importance and value of small Fellowship Groups. And we believe that God is leading us, for the spiritual good of the congregation, to develop them at All Souls. Indeed, so persuaded are we about this, that we mean to give them priority in the church's weekday programme. We hope that ultimately every member of the congregation will become a member of a Fellowship Group as well . . . Our desire is that each Fellowship Group will express and develop the three aspects of Christian fellowship which we find in Scripture, namely our relationship to God Himself, our care for one another and our service to the world. We hope and pray that the members of each group will increase in the knowledge of God by corporate devotional Bible reading, and will learn to care for one another in love and bear one another's burdens, and will engage together in some common Christian service.'

It may be helpful to see how the Fellowship Groups are attempting to fulfil this threefold ideal.

First, every Fellowship Group seeks to give expression to the common life which its members already enjoy, and to deepen and enrich it. The chief means to this end is devotional Bible reading and prayer. Every six months or so a suggested list of short Bible passages is produced, either consecutive or topical, sometimes with a few explanatory notes. This list is duplicated in sufficient quantity for every member to have a copy, so that some preparatory reading of the passage is possible. It is emphasized, however, that the Fellowship Group is not a

Bible study class, that the Bible reading must not therefore dominate the evening, and that the leader's responsibility is not to lecture the group. Instead, the task of the leaders (who are nearly all lay men and women) is to help the group to feed upon Christ together in and through His Word. Their object in reading is not just to understand what the passage means, but to go beyond its meaning to its message, to allow it to speak to our situation, to direct and correct us, to exhort, rebuke, challenge or comfort us. We emphasize that the reading of God's Word is never an end itself, but a means to a deeper knowledge of God Himself and to a more obedient conformity to His Will.

Many hazards threaten the profit of this Bible reading time. The garrulous have to be restrained and the dumb encouraged to speak. And the method of meditation has to be varied if monotony is to be avoided, now by looking through the passage verse by verse, now by selective reading, now by question and answer. Several leaders invite members of their group to take turns in leading. All try to encourage a relaxed, non-classroom atmosphere.

Once a year most of the Fellowship Groups receive Holy Communion in the room in which they meet. We have used a simple service in modern language, and the clergy have not worn robes. This has been a precious time of corporate feeding on Christ in sacrament as well as Scripture, since He makes Himself known to us not only in His Word, but also in the breaking of bread.

Most groups 'break bread' informally also, enjoying a simple form of 'agape' or 'love feast' each time they meet. In some cases it is only a cup of tea and a biscuit, in others it is a full meal. In either case the addition of the social to the spiritual tends to deepen the fellowship.

Secondly, the Fellowship Groups are seeking to extend their fellowship of 'sharing out' as well as of 'sharing in', for a Fellowship Group which is entirely inward-looking becomes ingrowing, unhealthy and sterile. Indeed, 'sharing in' and 'sharing out' belong together, and each becomes unbalanced without the other. Another way of putting the same thing is that the Christian is called both to 'holiness' and to 'worldliness', both to withdrawal and to involvement. Further, fruitful Christian involvement in the world is impossible without the spiritual resources which withdrawal supplies, while these resources (gained in withdrawal) are given to be expended in service in the world. Dr Elton Trueblood applies this truth to the church's common life. He defines the Church as 'a fellowship of consciously inadequate persons who gather because they are weak, and scatter to serve because their unity with one another and with Christ has made them bold'.[1] Again, 'we are making a great step forward when we realize that there is no inevitable contradiction between the idea of the scattered church and the idea of the gathered church. We gather in order to scatter!'[2]

What service, then, do Fellowship Groups perform? To begin with, each group is engaged in intercession, which can rightly be understood a⸗ common service, reaching out in prayer to embrace the whole world. This was emphasized in the policy statement already mentioned: 'during each Fellowship Group ... there will be a half-hour of prayer, stimulated and guided ... by parochial and missionary prayer topics. Some people have spoken with regret of the death of the Hour of Prayer, which for years has been the church's most important midweek meeting. This is more than understandable. The Council emphasize, however, that what is proposed is only the transformation of a particular form of prayer service into something else and something better. It will mean not the death of prayer, but rather its resurrection. Under the new scheme, many more people will, in fact, be praying than before. Moreover, the praying will be more audible, more natural, more intimate, and therefore, we believe, more effective. Let there be no mistake about it: we still intend

---

[1] Trueblood: *The Incendiary Fellowship*, p. 31
[2] Trueblood: *The Incendiary Fellowship*, p. 83

to put prayer first, and we believe that our serious intercession as a congregation is going in future to be considerably increased, improved and enriched.'

I think we can claim that this has proved to be true. One elderly and experienced man of prayer has described the change as 'a real blessing to the whole congregation'. A list of suggested prayer topics is duplicated each fortnight, relating to the work of the church and parish. In most groups these are read out by a member, while the rest listen or take notes, but a few groups like all their members to have the duplicated sheet so that they may take it home with them afterwards and continue to use it in their private prayers. Several have said that these topics give them 'inside information' about the life of the church and help them to feel more personally involved in it.

Then there is missionary prayer. Each Fellowship Group has 'adopted' one or two of our church's missionaries. Group members correspond with them and receive the magazine of their missionary society, so as to keep themselves up to date with news from the field. This arrangement has resulted in the formation of really personal bonds between missionaries and the supporting home church. One group has also made and dispatched needed items to a missionary in Uganda, and another has sent books to a missionary who works in a Bible Institute in Chile.

But we are not content for a Fellowship Group's common service to be limited to intercessory prayer. We believe it should be more than this. It is perhaps easiest for those groups which are composed of people who already work together – whether as visitors, Sunday School teachers or club leaders. Again, when the group is composed of local residents, it is natural for them to become concerned for and involved in the welfare of others living in the same street or block. This has happened with a few of our groups. For example one group, instead of their usual time of fellowship, spent an evening redecorating the flat of an old-age pensioner. But most of our groups have an eclectic membership and seek other avenues of service. It must be admitted that several have been unsuccessful – through lack of time or of enterprise. Others, however, have offered their practical services as a group – in the annual springclean of the church, in the door-to-door distribution of leaflets, in street 'fishing' before an evening service, in supporting an open-air service and in a visiting 'blitz' in another parish. Several groups have also made themselves responsible for the preparing of food, the waiting and the washing up at a parish function – including a Christmas party for overseas visitors, tea-parties for confirmation candidates and university freshers, a residential Family Service weekend and a number of Parish Evenings. Another group has started a 'self-denial' campaign, to stimulate practical concern for the needy people of the world. Certainly without some such common concern and service, the fellowship of any Christian group is maimed.

The third aspect of *koinonia*, sharing with one another, is probably the most difficult to achieve and develop. But if Christians are brothers and sisters in Christ, they should know each other, love each other, take an interest in each other and care for each other. As Bruce Larson has put it: 'The Church is meant to be a company of people as committed to one another as to Christ.'[1] This was an essential part of the Methodist class meetings. John Wesley wrote in his *Plain Account of the People called Methodists*:

> It can scarce be conceived what advantages have been reaped from this little prudential regulation. Many now happily experienced that Christian fellowship of which they had not so much as an idea before. They began to 'bear one another's burdens' and naturally to 'care for each other'. As they had daily a more intimate acquaintance with, so they had a more endeared affection for, each other. And 'speaking the truth in love, they grew up into Him in all things who is the Head, even Christ; from whom the whole body, fitly joined together, and compacted by that which every joint supplied, according to the effectual working in the measure of every part, increased unto the edifying of itself in love'.[2]

[1] Larson: *Dare To Live Now!*, p. 122
[2] quoted in J. S. Simon: *John Wesley and the Methodist Societies* (1923), p. 312-313

George Whitefield writes similarly in his *Letter to the Religious Societies*:

> My brethren . . . let us plainly and freely tell one another what God has done for our souls. To this end, you would do well, as others have done, to form yourselves into little companies of four or five each, and meet once a week to tell each other what is in your hearts; that you may then also pray for and comfort each other as need shall require. None but those who have experienced it can tell the unspeakable advantages of such a union and communion of souls. . . . None I think that truly loves his own soul and his brethren as himself, will be shy of opening his heart, in order to have their advice, reproof, admonition and prayers, as occasions require. A sincere person will esteem it one of the greatest blessings.

What Wesley and Whitefield wrote is undoubtedly true, but even sincere persons are sometimes shy, and may find it difficult to be open. In a questionnaire which I recently issued to Fellowship Group members, a number spoke of their personal reserve, and some indicated that they felt 'the climate of confidence' was missing which would make such an intimate exchange possible. Indeed, it must be confessed, some groups have acquiesced in the difficulties and abandoned the attempt to foster such sharing. Others, however, have persevered and have been rewarded. One member has written of 'the bonds of love and *genuine* interest and concern which have grown up between members over the months'. Another refers to the 'mutual assistance' he has found; he likens his group to 'a rock climber's rope'. Another describes the members of the group to which she belongs as 'now closely knit together as a family'. In answer to the question 'what have you found most helpful in your Fellowship Group?', several have referred to the opportunity to share their thoughts and problems, their doubts and fears, together with blessings received and lessons learned, and one specified 'the certainty that the members really care for each other'.

So whenever the Fellowship Group meets, the leader is encouraged to make time for an expression of this part of Christian fellowship. Members are given the opportunity to share what is on their heart. In the questionnaire I asked: 'can you give any example of the group bearing or sharing one of your burdens?' Many could. Several had been prayed for and visited during a period of sickness. Others appreciated the sympathy and prayers of the group in a time of bereavement and loneliness. One could say regarding a time of adversity: 'they covered me with prayer in various ways'. Others had asked for specific prayer regarding an exam, a new job, the possibility of God's call to be a missionary, the need for accommodation or staff, or some Christian service they were undertaking. A doctor was supported by his group when giving a series of addresses at a Christian medical conference, and a girl while she worked at a holiday camp. Others have shared with their group their concern for sick relatives, and for friends or colleagues they were longing to win for Christ. One group was able to report four conversions among friends and relatives of its members, in answer to their united intercession. It may be said, therefore, that this ideal of 'caring and sharing', and of 'bearing one another's burdens', is beginning to be fulfilled. It cannot be artificially induced. But as mutual love grows in a group, mutual care grows with it.

Of course what Wesley called a 'prudential regulation' is also a perilous procedure. It exposes frail sinners to the dangers of exhibitionism, hypocrisy and self-pity. But there is safety in numbers – in a Fellowship Group as in a family. There's nothing like a family to knock off our rough corners. They will sympathize with us and stand by us loyally when we are in genuine trouble. But they will stand no nonsense if they think we are trying to exploit them!

THE IDEAL AND THE REALITY

Fellowship Groups are composed of human beings, and all human beings differ from one another. We have no desire, therefore, to stereotype a group's programme or development. Nevertheless we believe that true Christian *koinonia* involves the rich and comprehensive sharing which I have tried to unfold. And therefore we constantly keep before our eyes the threefold biblical ideal. We are anxious that the groups will not become unbalanced and degenerate into being merely Bible reading groups or prayer groups or study groups. We want them to be true to their name, 'fellowship groups' expressing the fulness of Christian fellowship. So we keep asking ourselves: are we growing in Christian maturity together? Are we serving the Lord, the Church or the world together? Are we increasing in love and care for one another?

'I think the groups are the nucleus and heart of the church', one member wrote. This we increasingly believe, and so try to keep them in the forefront of our thinking. Every person who joins the church is given details of Fellowship Groups and encouraged to join one. And every new Christian who graduates from a Nursery Class is urged to go on to a Fellowship Group.

So each group is seeking to become what Hendrik Kraemer in his book several times calls 'a Christocentric, Christocratic brotherhood'. But even if Christ is the unseen centre and leader of the group, it still needs a human leader. Generally speaking, these are lay people, while members of the church staff circulate, trying to attend a different group every fortnight. This lay leadership of the groups makes possible that delegated *episcope* (pastoral oversight), which we have already seen to be so desirable. Do the lay people resent the lay leadership? Far from it! We pastors may cherish the illusion that we are needed and missed, but the groups consider that they get on better without us! In the questionnaire I asked: 'are you in favour of the lay leadership of the groups?' 95 out of the 108 who answered were in favour. They gave three main reasons. The first was biblical principle, that lay leaders 'are sharing in the ministry of the church', that 'the gift of spiritual leadership is not conferred by ordination', that such experience 'helps to develop the spiritual abilities of the laity', and that 'this makes us more aware that we are the church'. The second was pastoral necessity, that the clergy do not have time to exercise all the leadership and must therefore share it. And the third reason was rather embarrassingly personal. Lay leaders, the questionnaire answers inform us, are 'more human and understanding', particularly because they are themselves living and working in lay situations. Further, as a Korean girl put it candidly, 'if clergy-man leads group I become selfconscious and reserved'. 33 people confessed that they are much more free, relaxed and at ease in the absence of the clergy!

Conclusion

It is very necessary for the health and vigour of the contemporary Church that it should recover the biblical emphasis which we have been exploring. The principles of it can no doubt be applied in a multitude of different ways. But the principles themselves are of permanent validity and cannot be changed. They are also closely related to each other and cannot be separated – at least not without resultant damage to the Church's life.

First, God's people are one holy people, owing their unity and holiness to the will and call of God Himself. They are His *ecclesia*, called out to be His. As such, they are distinct from the world, but essentially undifferentiated from one another.

Next, in this one *ecclesia* God appoints different men (and women) to different ministries. Each has his particular *diakonia* to perform. And the principal service of the ordained ministry is to serve the rest of the Church, proclaiming Christ by word and sacrament, 'warning every man and teaching every man in all wisdom, that we may present every man mature in Christ'.[1] So the clergy may say to the laity, '*our* God-given *diakonia* in the Church is to help to equip you for *your* God-given *diakonia* in the world'.

Further, although the *diakonia* of God's people (that is the laity) is varied, one of its highest forms is *marturia*, witness. Living and working in the midst of the secular world, the layman is in the front line of the Church's testimony.

To this work of witness all God's people are summoned, and are regularly strengthened in the doing of it by their *koinonia*, their common share in Christian privilege and responsibility.

[1] Colossians 1.28

Select Bibliography

SOME recent works, which relate to the theology of the laity and which are quoted in this book, are detailed below. They are listed in alphabetical order according to the authors' names. You are referred to this list also for works for which only brief details are given in the footnotes or the text.

Tom Allan: *The Face Of My Parish* (SCM Press, 1954)

Kathleen Bliss: *We The People, A Book About Laity* (SCM Press, 1963)

Kenneth Chafin: *Help! I'm A Layman* (Word Books, 1966)

Archbishop Cyril Garbett: *The Claims Of The Church Of England* (Hodder and Stoughton, 1947)

George Goyder: *The People's Church* (Hodder and Stoughton, 1966)

Michael Green: *Called To Serve—Ministry and Ministers in the Church* (Hodder and Stoughton, 1964)

Sir Kenneth Grubb: *A Layman Looks At The Church* (Hodder and Stoughton, 1964)

Hendrik Kraemer: *A Theology Of The Laity* (Lutterworth, 1958)

Bruce Larson: *Dare To Live Now!* (Michigan, Zondervan, 1965)

Keith Miller: *The Taste Of New Wine* (Word Books, 1963)

Lesslie Newbigin: *The Household Of God* (SCM Press, 1953)

J. A. T. Robinson and others: *Layman's Church* (Lutterworth, 1963)

J. A. T. Robinson: *The New Reformation?* (SCM Press, 1965)

Elton Trueblood: *The Incendiary Fellowship* (Harper and Row, 1967)

Stephen Verney: *Fire In Coventry* (Hodder and Stoughton, 1964)

M. A. C. Warren: *Revival – An Enquiry* (SCM Press, 1954)

Reports (listed chronologically)

Towards the Conversion of England (Press and Publications Board of the Church Assembly, 1945)

The Evanston Report, the official report of the Second Assembly of the
    World Council of Churches (SCM Press, 1955)
The Lambeth Conference 1958 (SPCK, 1958)
Keele '67, the National Evangelical Anglican Congress Statement
    (Falcon, 1967)
The Documents of Vatican II, edited by Walter M. Abbott, SJ (Geoffrey
    Chapman, 1967)
The Lambeth Conference 1968 (SPCK, 1968)

46256